The
KIDULT
HANDBOOK

From Blanket Forts to
Capture the Flag, a Grownup's
Guide to Playing Like a Kid

Nicole Booz

ADAMS MEDIA

NEW YORK   LONDON   TORONTO   SYDNEY   NEW DELHI

To Jon

Aadamsmedia

Adams Media
An Imprint of Simon & Schuster, Inc.
57 Littlefield Street
Avon, Massachusetts 02322

First Adams Media trade paperback edition May 2018

ADAMS MEDIA and colophon are trademarks of Simon & Schuster.

For information about special discounts for bulk purchases, please contact Simon & Schuster Special Sales at 1-866-506-1949 or business@simonandschuster.com.

The Simon & Schuster Speakers Bureau can bring authors to your live event. For more information or to book an event contact the Simon & Schuster Speakers Bureau at 1-866-248-3049 or visit our website at www.simonspeakers.com.

Interior design by Katrina Machado
Interior images © 123RF/artur80b; Getty Images/Sudowoodo; -VICTOR-

Manufactured in the United States of America

10 9 8 7 6 5 4 3 2

Library of Congress Cataloging-in-Publication Data has been applied for.

ISBN 978-1-5072-0758-1
ISBN 978-1-5072-0759-8 (ebook)

Acknowledgments

First of all, I'd like to thank Cate Prato and the team at Adams Media for making this book the most fun a kidult could have.

A massive thank you to my husband, Jon, for the endless support and iced lattes. To my mom, Travis, Emily, Robin, and my in-laws for believing in my dreams.

To my hype squad—Beatrix, Brooke, Charissa, Erin, Gina, Katie, Kristin, Lindsey, Marina, Michelle, and Tori—you are the best support system I could ever ask for. And to Jacquie O. for always doing the most and inspiring me beyond measure.

Finally, to the *GenTwenty* team—your passion and talent illuminate the world.

CONTENTS

5

INTRODUCTION

Adulting is hard! Paying bills, maintaining your car, buying groceries (again)—it's enough to make you want to close your eyes and wish you were still a kid. Fortunately, *kidulting* allows you to indulge your inner child in the best way possible. What's kidulting? It's letting go—for a little while—of the work/errands/responsibilities of adulthood in playful and nostalgic ways. Kidulting takes you back to an easier time when you had fewer worries and a beginner's mind—a Zen concept that refers to being fresh, curious, and open to possibilities. When you were a kid, you had beginner's mind in abundance. Every day you learned something new and every experience, no matter how basic, brought wonder and excitement. Splashing in the rain. Looking up at the stars. Blowing bubbles. Carefree days!

Can you remember the last time you did something just for the joy of it, instead of having to be an expert? I can't be the only one struggling to pull off that trick.

Throughout *The Kidult Handbook* you'll find 160 activities that encourage you to access your beginner's mind, look at life with fresh eyes, and *play*. These fun and creative ideas give you everything you need to step away from the "real world," relieve stress, bust out some endorphins, boost your immune system, indulge in some kid-style treats, and—dare I say it?—get happy.

To help you find your best kidult experiences, I've grouped the activities into seven sections: A Beginner's Mind, Do with Friends, You're Never Too Old For..., Party, Party, Party, Field Day Extravaganza, A Camping We Will Go, and The Great Escape. So, let's take a look at what each section includes!

First up: A Beginner's Mind. Imagination is vital to growing as a person and bringing fresh ideas to your work. But when was the last time you let your imagination run wild? Playing like a kid helps open your mind up to new possibilities. In this section you'll find all kinds of games and activities to set your imagination free and stimulate your brain to learn and grow. Taking on a physics challenge straight out of 6th grade, playing with LEGOs, or crafting with paper and scissors are all ways to look anew at things we take for granted as adults.

 Speaking of friends, how do you keep up with old friendships and start new ones when you're so busy adulting? And, by "keep up" I mean do things together IRL, not just via group chat. I've got that covered for you, too, in Do with Friends. Make friend-time fun and memorable with games like Bingo and get-togethers like an Adult-Mixer Scavenger Hunt. On a warm summer day, head outside to track down the ice cream truck, or get a group together to make slime or Dunkaroos.

A big part of kidulting is remembering that You're Never Too Old For...pretty much anything. In this section, I encourage you to live in a treehouse (temporarily), find an adult-friendly playground or trampoline park, and touch a starfish. And be sure to Party, Party, Party, with games from your childhood or activities that combine kiddie and grown-up ideas of fun, like Quidditch Pong and making alcoholic ice pops.

Laughing is not only a great way to relieve stress but it helps improve your immune system and cope with pain too. While adults may be short on LOLs, kids can always find something to laugh at, whether it's a dad joke or acting silly. In *The Kidult Handbook*, you'll find tons of activities to do with friends and family that will have you laughing your crazy socks off! In fact, you can plan an entire Field Day Extravaganza with the games and challenges I've provided, sparking guffaws and giggles, not to mention helping you stay in shape. (Oh so much more fun when you "play" instead of "exercise.")

And what about creativity? From finger painting to tie dyeing, kidults are encouraged to get messy and hands on. Anything goes! Nowadays, only some of us have creative day jobs (looking at you, social media marketers) or time for hobbies that regularly lead to artsy fun. You'll learn how to make time for artistic expression and kick that creativity up a notch with the DIY arts and crafts ideas you'll find under A Camping We Will Go and The Great Escape. That last section is also where you'll find ideas for zoning out alone—inside a blanket fort or lying back on the grass, watching the clouds go by.

To help you find the fun, each activity comes with a key telling you the Game Setup (Indoors, Outdoors), Bank (cost: $ = $0-25, $$ = $26-50, $$$ = $51+), and Number of Players (). But keep in mind that each activity is flexible and costs can vary depending on your location.

If this all seems rather silly, then you really need this book! Embrace your childhood memories, activities, and favorite munchables with open arms. Not only will acting like a kid again bring you joy and relieve stress, it will help you become a better adult. If you want to get the most out of these crazy, kidult challenges, you need to sharpen those communication skills, put yourself out there, and (last, but not least) read the room! That's kidulting at its finest.

So, what are you waiting for? Pop the popcorn, grab your laser tag gear, and make every day the best day ever. Let's kidult!

PART 1
A BEGINNER'S MIND

A beginner's mind. *What does that mean?* you wonder. (You're off to a great start!) Think of your beginner's mind as almost like a blank slate. As a child you know very little about the world around you, but you learn more every day through logic and reasoning. Instead of binge-watching yet another mindless TV show, these all-time-fave kidulting activities will keep you creating and innovating like a kid genius to keep your mind flexible and strong. Solving these problems and winning the game will give you a much-needed confidence boost. You can say, "I've totally got this!" and mean it.

You'll be tapping into activities from childhood, when you had no preconceived notions about how the world works. Through unique challenges and games you'll easily access your beginner's mind and in doing so, strengthen those logic and reasoning skills that you haven't used in a while. What could be more fun than reminiscing on childhood favorites to feel young again? It's time you get back to stoking your curious fires.

Act Out

$$$ | 👤+👤👤👤👤 | 🌳🏠

Bring out your inner queen—or just pretend to be one onstage—by enrolling in a beginner's acting class. The long hours spent memorizing lines will be worth it after you nail the performance and leave the crowd in stitches!

Acting gives you the chance to step out of your own life, even if just for a moment, to be someone completely different. And who hasn't dreamed of that? In one production you might be a pauper during the Renaissance, and in another you could find yourself portraying a pirate in the South China Sea. You might not end up with a star on the Hollywood Walk of Fame, but that's okay! No role is too big or too small for you to conquer.

If you thought the best thing about acting is that you get to be someone else, think again. The best thing starts with the camaraderie among your fellow cast mates that comes from late nights of working together to mark scenes, build backdrops, and create clever costumes.

Even if you fall flat, the show must go on!

Play with LEGOs

After a long day at the office, the first thing you want to do is head straight for the couch and turn on *Netflix* to finish last night's episode. But doesn't giving your eyes a break from the binge-watching sound like a much-needed reprieve? Head to a local toy store and grab a few LEGO sets (or raid your parents' garage—there's bound to be tubs of LEGO pieces hanging around in there somewhere).

The name LEGO comes from *leg godt*, a Danish phrase that translates to "play well." And that's exactly what you're going to do. Let your imagination wander as you put together the pieces. What will you build today?

Get creative! Two LEGO pieces can be combined twenty-four different ways. When you throw just four more into the mix, that number shoots up to an impressive 915 million ways. With all those combinations, there's really no limit to all the wondrous things you can make with LEGOs. Surprise your pals when you host game night with your new LEGO coffee table. Bonus points if you make matching chairs too.

★ PRO TIP ★

Make sure you clean up after yourself—a LEGO to the foot is way more painful in adulthood. Ouch.

FUN FOR EVERYONE

LEGOs have been standardized since the 1950s—meaning LEGOs from the '50s are compatible with the LEGOs you can buy today. Far out.

Do the Physics Egg Challenge

Remember when you thought you'd never need to use the equation *force = mass × acceleration* again? Well, today's the day you and your friends are going to have a physics competition that will have you cracking up. That sneaky bit of knowledge from science class will help you in the noblest of pursuits: saving a helpless egg. Your job is to design a container that houses an egg and keeps it safe when dropped from a two-story window.

The catch here is that you're only allowed to use two materials: straws and masking tape. If that's too easy for you, Kid Genius, make it more difficult by using paper instead of straws. Get even more creative and work together in teams to build a container that can keep an egg safe using only supplies found in the kitchen.

You'll have a blast competing against your friends and family to save an egg when you've outgrown Easter baskets. (Chocolate bunnies are for all ages, though!) Don't let it get you down if your egg cracks. You can really make an impact with this one! I'll see myself out.

Do Some Deducing with Guess Who?

$ $ $ | 👤👤👤👤👤+ | 🌳🏠

The classic version of Guess Who? from your childhood is a two-player board game that uses yes/no questions to deduce which character the opposing player has selected. Of course, the first player to guess correctly takes home the trophy (and all the bragging rights).

This version of Guess Who? requires you to play double duty and be both the sneak and the investigator.

To start, have everyone in your group write down one secret fact about themselves. Put all the folded sheets of paper in a hat or bowl. Take turns pulling out a fact and reading it aloud to the crowd. During a turn, each person gets to ask three yes/no questions to the group to narrow down which player the fact describes.

You'll be able to deduce some information easily—for example, you can see who has brown hair and you might already know who vacationed in Hawaii last winter. Beyond that, however, you'll have to ask questions in order to narrow down the target. Good luck, Sherlock!

Make Paper Chains

When it comes to cheap and easy decorations, paper chains are a go-to. Need to decorate your office for a holiday? Paper chain. Need quick and festive decor for a bridal shower? Paper chain. Throwing in to spruce up your kid's classroom? Paper chain.

Some might call them basic, and they'd be right. But kidult paper chains go to the next level. Instead of just strips of paper, go for red heart-shaped links for a gorgeous Valentine's theme. Christmas trees or green wreaths are perfect for the holidays and brown or yellow leaves are great for fall. Go all out and use glitter paper, scrapbooking paper, even old notes or schoolwork to match the theme of your party. With your imagination, the choices are endless!

To make a paper chain, start by cutting your paper into strips. Take one of the strips and put it end to end and tape it together to create a circle. Then, pick up a second strip of paper and loop it through the first circle you've created. Put those ends together to create another circle, therefore interconnecting the circles. Continue in this way until you reach the desired length or until you run out of paper.

Next time you're decorating for an event with friends, turn paper chains into an office competition to really bring out everyone's creative side. If you're up for a challenge, see who can make the longest paper chain out of one sheet of paper or who can make the most creative paper chain without using scissors. Have fun!

Do the Marble Challenge

Let's face it, team-building activities can be boring and downright exhausting. Spice them up with a challenge that gets more fun with every round. Make sure to call dibs on the most engineering-oriented friend before the games begin!

To play, each team will need ten marbles, a 12" piece of string, five rubber bands, and two cups. Keep your teams small to prevent the game from getting out of hand. Pro tip: spend more time moving the marbles instead of arguing strategy—this isn't your 2 p.m. meeting, people!

Have each team start with ten marbles in one cup. The goal is to move all the marbles from one cup to the other without touching either the marbles or the cups with your hands. The catch? You're only allowed to use the piece of string and rubber bands to complete the task. This is your chance to be the hero you've always wanted to be. Don't let me down!

Shut Up and Dance with Me

Moving your body across the dance floor and sweating out the stress from the week is the best way to spend a Saturday morning. Round up a fearless group of friends and your leg warmers and hit the studio for a fun-filled hour of new moves before hitting your favorite spot for bottom-less mimosas. Getting yourself into first position before brunch will get your heart rate up and send your confidence soaring!

Many dance studios these days offer adult-only classes for all skill levels. You don't even have to come dressed in a leotard and tights—unless you want to of course. Grab your partner and go swing dancing, sign up for salsa, or try your feet at the waltz. It's like *Dancing with the Stars* for newbies. You're the star of the show in this scenario. When it comes to dance, there's something that everyone can enjoy. You're going to have a blast groovin' around the dance floor!

Quick, Improv It

Are you quick on your feet? The best way to find out is to lend your voice to an improv class. Improv encourages spontaneity and creativity through unscripted performance. It might seem scary at first, but it's a lot of fun once you get the hang of it. It is based on the "yes, and..." method, which goes like this: what one person says is accepted as true (yes), the next person should expand and continue on that line of thinking (and...).

Trying your hand at improv opens up your mind and teaches you how to communicate and collaborate. Whether you're an introvert or an extrovert, you're going to find yourself in some interesting situations in these classes.

Believe it or not, this "yes, and..." technique is frequently used in professional environments to improve the brainstorming process. It's true! When people bounce ideas off of one another in this way it breaks down barriers and fosters the expansion and sharing of ideas. Having this skill comes in handy when you're trying to stand out in a positive way.

If diving headfirst into an improv class is too far out of your comfort zone, give it a go in your next team meeting. Using the "yes, and..." technique, you might find that Bob's idea might not be so bad after all. (At the very least you can try to make it worthwhile. I won't tell!)

March Some Ants on a Log

$\$\$\$$ | 👤+👥👥👥👥 | 🌳🏠

Ants on a Log is one of the simplest recipes you will ever make. You only need three ingredients and a few minutes to prepare this treat. Not only that, but they are cute and nutritious.

Consider this basic snack to be brain food for all your logic-improving activities from this section!

MAKES 1 SERVING

YOU'LL NEED:

- 3 large stalks celery, trimmed and cut into thirds
- 3 tablespoons creamy peanut butter
- 3 tablespoons raisins

DIRECTIONS:

1. Fill the hollow part of each celery stalk with even amounts of peanut butter to create the "logs."
2. Sprinkle raisins on top of the peanut butter on each section as the "ants." Enjoy!

Play Twenty Questions

Is it found on our planet? Does it breathe? Was it born before 1900? Can you buy it at the grocery store? Can you walk inside of it? Does it cost more than $100? Do you have to feed it? Is it bigger than a pair of glasses? Think hard—you've only got twelve questions left to narrow it down!

A rousing game of Twenty Questions is a thrilling way to take your sleuthing skills to the next level. It's challenging, fun, and requires hardly any equipment.

To play, one person comes up with a noun (person, place, or thing) and writes it down on a piece of paper, and then folds up the answer and stashes it away for safekeeping—this keeps everyone honest. The ultimate goal of the game is to guess the noun. The catch is you can only ask twenty questions to figure it out. Get it right and you win! Get it wrong and it's game over. If you're able to guess the answer in less than twenty questions, you're the master of deductive reasoning.

The next time you're on a road trip heading to a beach paradise, challenge your group to a game of Twenty Questions and see who's the trickiest of them all.

Play Sudoku

Sharpen your pencils, sharpen your mind—it's time to put those problem-solving skills to good use! Sudoku is a single-player logic game that calls on your deductive reasoning to solve the pattern. But you don't have to be a rocket scientist to solve this one, folks. Each row, column, 3" × 3" square, and 9" × 9" grid will contain the numbers 1 through 9 with no repeats. It's up to you to find where each number belongs.

Playing games like sudoku allows you to use your mind in new and different ways. The only way you grow is by challenging yourself to step outside of your comfort zone and try new things—and that includes the ways you think. In this game you're forced to see patterns, use deductive reasoning, and think ahead to solve the grid.

Whether you're a beginner or an expert, there are countless sudoku puzzles available in varying levels of difficulty at Sudoku.com. Challenge yourself to complete one sudoku puzzle each day for the next week just for fun!

Get Jiggy(saw) with It

$$$ | 👤+👤👤👤👤 | 🌳🏠

Challenge your squad with a monstrous jigsaw puzzle. I'm talking one with hundreds or thousands of pieces that would take you weeks to put together on your own. Approach it with a spirit of cooperation. ("Hey, this piece looks like it goes with part of your sky" rather than "Excuse me, that's *my* piece!") Keep the snacks coming and trade sections when people start to get frustrated. It'll also be fun to relive memories of when you all did that giant puzzle. In fact, you could make it an annual event. It's teamwork that makes the dream work, after all!

If the size isn't enough of a challenge for you, hide the cover image while you're putting the pieces together. This ups the ante because you have no idea if you're hot or cold when determining where pieces go. Good luck!

?? POP TRIVIA ??

The world's largest jigsaw puzzle available for purchase is Ravensburger's 40,320-piece whopper. Suddenly a 1,000-piece puzzle seems completely manageable.

Ask, "Would You Rather...?"

$$$ | ♟♟ + ♟♟♟ | ♣ ⌂

Would you rather always be busy or always be bored?

These are the types of questions you'll be answering in a round of Would You Rather. You'll have to carefully weigh the pros and cons of either two very desirable or two very undesirable options.

Of course, it all happens in the hypothetical, so you don't need to worry about the consequences of your choices—unlike that fifth beer last night. However, the game does make you think about what your true preferences are. Plus, it's fun to see what other people think too!

Here are a few starter ideas to get you going:

Would you rather...

- Eat slugs or eat spiders?
- See free movies for the rest of your life or get free food at one restaurant for the rest of your life?
- Have to bike everywhere or walk everywhere?
- Run a marathon or take the LSAT?
- Drink only alcohol for the rest of your life or drink no alcohol for the rest of your life?
- Only be able to tell the truth or only be able to tell lies?
- Have 3" fingernails or 3" toenails?
- Have a vacation home in the Bahamas or a vacation home in Italy?
- Go to the moon or go to Mars?

Whip Up a Chocolate Peanut Butter Breakfast Smoothie

Breakfast is the most important meal of the day. So it should include chocolate, right? Maybe not, but who's gonna stop you? Actually, this low-sugar, high-protein recipe makes a lot of sense nutritionally. It's quick, easy, and basically tastes like dessert for breakfast. And did I mention it has chocolate in it?

MAKES 1 SERVING

YOU'LL NEED:

- ¹/₂ frozen banana
- ¹/₂ tablespoon cocoa powder
- 1 tablespoon peanut butter
- 1 cup milk
- 1 cup ice
- Optional: 2 tablespoons vanilla yogurt

DIRECTIONS:

1. Add all the ingredients to a blender and pulse until smooth.
2. Pour into a cup and serve. Good morning!

Challenge Your Memory

Is your memory in tip-top shape? There's one way to find out! Sometimes referred to as Concentration, Memory Match is a card game that puts your short-term memory to the test.

You can buy decks with images on them, but you can easily play with a regular deck of fifty-two cards. In this case, you'll want to match the red cards together and the black cards together to find complementary matches.

To play, mix up a deck of cards and lay them all facedown in front of you. Flip over two cards at a time. Your goal is to find cards that match. If they do match, congrats! You either have beginner's luck or a promising memory. (Sure, it's definitely the latter.)

For example, if you're using a regular deck of playing cards, you'll match the eight of hearts with the eight of diamonds. The key to the game is to remember where the cards have been laid out. Only two cards can be face up at any given time. Once you've located a matching pair, remove those cards from play and continue until no cards remain.

Pair up your kid and their friends (or grandparents) to see who is able to find the most matches! Step it up by setting a timer when playing alone. With 3 minutes on the clock, you're racing against yourself to see if you can find all the matches before time runs out. If not, it's game over.

Settle It with Rock, Paper, Scissors

It's the age-old question: where should we go for dinner? You're jonesin' for taco Tuesday at your favorite Mexican spot while your roommate wants to stay in and order takeout from the new pizza place down the street. How will you ever decide? Take out a fist and count to three... Wait, where did you think I was going with this? Rock, Paper, Scissors is the classic decision-maker that will have you on your way in no time, no matter what you're trying to pick between.

Rock, Paper, Scissors has a clear winner and a clear loser, unless there is a tie—in which case you go again to break the tie. Many people go for "best two out of three" or "best three out of five." That way not one single game determines a winner or a loser and each player has a better chance of coming out on top. (And ultimately deciding whether you'll be having Mexican or pizza.) To settle the debate, the participants use their hand to indicate a rock, scissors, or paper. The rock is formed by making a fist, paper is an outstretched, flat hand, and scissors is done by holding out your pointer and middle finger, like a peace sign. Rock beats scissors; scissors beats paper; and paper beats rock. If the two players make the same choice, a tie is called and another round is played. It's game on!

The next time you need to decide on what you're having for dinner or who goes first, don't waste time arguing over who it should be. Use the method you employed when you were a kid to solve the conundrum.

Play Board Games

Friday night is here and you're set up with your popcorn sitting cross-legged hashing out rules with your BFF. You're ready to start passing go and collecting $200 as you buy and build up the entire right side of the Monopoly board. Houses and hotels, you want it all! Do you have what it takes to get there?

Board games such as Risk, Monopoly, and Settlers of Catan put our critical thinking skills to the ultimate test by challenging us to think a few moves ahead and strategize with (or against) other players to take over the world. I mean, to win the game.

If you've ever played any of these games, you already know it's not as simple as it seems to come out on top. Winning or losing is about developing a cunning strategy that outwits your opponents. Some games are about speedy action and getting ahead while others encourage a slower, more laborious plan to win the game through calculated concessions and big victories. Thinking long-term and reacting quickly will keep you alive as you navigate these risky board games. You really never know what's going to happen, especially as you get more advanced.

No matter what you're planning, you'll need to bring your A game to the table!

PART 2
DO WITH FRIENDS (DWF)

The more the merrier when it comes to DWF (that's short for "do with friends"). Face it, everything is better when you're surrounded by the people you love most. When life gets busy with grown-up jobs and chaperoning afternoon soccer games for your own kids, those friend dates often get pushed to the back burner. And what a shame that is!

Whether you're catching up over brunch or spending a Saturday afternoon hanging out, time spent with friends is never wasted. In fact, it's actually really good for you! Friends makes you feel cared for, and laughing with people who "get you" is a powerful stress reliever. Get your squad together and make some new memories with the games, DIY activities, delicious recipes, and heart-pumping challenges in this section. Trust me, they will have you laughing your socks off. Whatever you end up doing, make sure you DWF!

Yell "Bingo!"

Bingo is old school—a definite throwback to middle school fundraisers or Wednesday nights down at the church hall. You can roll your eyes all you want, but admit it, you're on the edge of your seat waiting for the elusive five in a row, ready to shout "Bingo!" like you just won the March Madness pool. The next time you have friends over and don't feel like binge-watching *Netflix*, get a game of Bingo going. It's easy to play, easy to DIY, and provides a healthy dose of competition.

To DIY your own version at home, start by making a grid. A standard Bingo grid is 5" × 5"—five horizontal spaces for each letter of the word *Bingo* across the top and five verticals for each letter down the side. This leaves you with a table of twenty-five total spaces. Each player gets a "free space" anywhere on the board. Decide what to fill each space on your board with—numbers, pop icons or celebrities, cities or countries, or book titles are all fun options—and make sure everyone uses the same items (it's a good idea to have a printer and glue sticks handy). Have each player choose her own unique location for these and fill in her board with one per square. In total, there will be twenty-four items and one free space on each board.

One player will be the caller—i.e., the person who calls out the numbers or items as the game goes along. The caller should write down everything written on the players' boards, cut them out on individual pieces of paper, and then put them in a bowl to pull out one by one until a player shouts "Bingo!"

Use coins, pieces of candy, or even dry beans to mark the spaces as you go. Bingo happens when you fill five spaces in a row diagonally, vertically, or horizontally. The numbers or items are verified by the caller and then it's time for the next round. If you're feeling fancy, have a basket of small prizes (such as gift cards for coffee or scratch-off tickets) for the winners.

S-P-E-L-L-I-N-G B-E-E

In ancient times before autocorrect, we had to rely on "sounding it out" to spell a word correctly, and even then, that didn't always work! I know you give yourself an inner fist pump when you get a word right without technology stepping in (I know I do).

Hosting your own spelling bee is easy. Simply gather a group of friends and play elimination style until a champion remains. Have one person play judge and flip to random pages in a dictionary, choosing words as you go along. Alternatively, you can each pass the dictionary around using the same method so everyone can play. There are enough words and dictionary pages that you shouldn't have to worry about repeats happening. You get a point for spelling a word correctly and no points if you misspell the word. After ten rounds, the person with the most points wins the game.

Play elimination rounds competitive spelling bee style or just play for fun to improve your knowledge and test one another. And remember, no phones allowed!

?? POP TRIVIA ??

The Oxford English Dictionary (Second Edition) has twenty volumes and includes 171,476 main entries for words in current use (that doesn't even count the thousands of other listings, such as obsolete words). Whoa.

Run with an Adult–Mixer Scavenger Hunt

$$$ | ♦♦♦♦♦+ | ♣♦

Chatting about the weather has a time and place, but why not liven up the party with a curious scavenger hunt that makes the conversation interesting! The goal of this sleuthing activity is to find one person in the group who matches each description. You'll get to know people's backgrounds and experiences to promote a deeper, more meaningful connection by highlighting what you have in common. Naturally, there's some healthy competition involved—it's still a scavenger hunt after all!

Depending on the size of your group, make a list of ten to twenty-five items to "find." Following are a few ideas to inspire you. Give everyone a sheet of paper with the list of items and let them at it until someone wins. There's a catch, though: no name can appear on the list more than once.

1. Whose favorite color is blue?
2. Who has a twin or has twin siblings?
3. Who has traveled internationally in the past two weeks?
4. Who has traveled to New Orleans in the past year?
5. Who has two kids—one son and one daughter?
6. Whose hobby is fishing?
7. Who has run a marathon?
8. Who is vegan?
9. Whose favorite show is *Criminal Minds*?
10. Who married their high school sweetheart?

If no one is able to check everything off the list, the person with the highest number of matches wins the hunt. This is perfect for a big group, such as at your ten-year class reunion. Game on, people.

Try the "Try Not to Laugh Challenge"

$$$ | 👤👤👤👤👤+ | 🌳 🏠

You're sitting across from your BFF sticking out your tongue and cross-ing your eyes...and she's shaking trying to hold in her giggles. This is how you'll find yourself when you take on the Try Not to Laugh Challenge. There's nothing a little TNLC can't cure!

One of the best parts of childhood is that you're allowed to not have to take anything too seriously. Bills? Not your problem yet. Growing a career? Don't really have to worry about that either. Increased responsibil-ities come with getting older, so it is easy forget that it's okay to let loose!

In fact, laughing is one of the best ways to reduce stress and improve your overall well-being. The more you laugh, the more endorphins are released, and the more relaxed you feel. Even though laughing might not be on your official to-do list every day, it unofficially should be!

For the Try Not to Laugh Challenge, you and a friend sit across from each other and take 1-minute turns doing anything possible to make the other person laugh.

You can make the challenge more intense by reducing the time limit to 30 seconds. Or, limit the types of things you can do to make each other laugh. One version might include only telling jokes; another might include not speaking at all. It's totally up to you to decide how you want the challenge to go.

Hey, on second thought, this is a competition you might actually want to lose!

Dip Some Homemade Dunkaroos

For the most part you're into eating clean and focusing on "good" carbs, but sometimes you just really need a little something to make a bad day better ASAP. If no one's around to give you a hug, a favorite childhood treat will do the trick. That familiar taste brings back childhood memories and makes you feel safe and secure.

Case in point: Dunkaroos. Eating Dunkaroos was a science. It was crucial to ration your dips of each cookie in the icing. Otherwise, you risked running out of icing long before you ran out of cookies. The key is to have enough icing for each cookie, or if you're like me, save enough icing to have one loaded cookie at the end. Delicious.

Sadly, these sweet treats aren't easily available for purchase anymore, but luckily they're unbelievably simple to make!

MAKES 16 SERVINGS

YOU'LL NEED:

- 1 (15-ounce) box cake mix (Funfetti is the standard, but get creative)
- 1 (8-ounce) container Cool Whip
- 1 cup plain yogurt
- Optional: sprinkles
- Animal crackers, graham crackers, or Teddy Grahams for dipping

FUN FOR EVERYONE.

If Dunkaroos aren't your thing, go for home-made Hostess CupCakes or old-school milk and cookies. Yum.

DIRECTIONS:

1. Mix together the cake mix, Cool Whip, yogurt, and sprinkles (if using) in a large bowl. You can eat the mixture right away or refrigerate it until you're ready to go. (Please teach me your ways.)
2. Get out your icing vehicles for dipping and dunk away. Enjoy!

Spread Out a DIY Sundae Bar

For a sweet end to a day of hiking, biking, or gaming with friends, head to the bar—the sundae bar, that is. Relaxing with friends while enjoying ice cream is sure to brighten your mood not just during the summer, but anytime of the year. A DIY sundae bar is the perfect addition to any of the games and activities you'll find in this chapter.

Have everyone bring their favorite toppings and line them up on a counter. Pick up some vanilla ice cream, or chocolate if that's more your thing, and have everyone DIY their own delicious sundaes and then retire to the porch to enjoy the sun or laze around a cozy fire.

The topping combinations are endless. You could have your favorite candies, such as Snickers, M&M's, Oreos, or Reese's. For the adventurous among you, throw fruity candy such as Nerds, Skittles, or gummy bears into the mix. Of course you can't forget the traditional toppings as well, such as sprinkles (or jimmies), hot fudge or butterscotch, whipped cream, and a cherry for the top.

Too indulgent? Include fruit in your sundae bar. Bananas, straw-berries, and raspberries all complement ice cream—or low-fat frozen yogurt—well.

I'll bring the waffle cones!

Hunt Down the Ice Cream Truck

It's great that you've resigned yourself to cutting back on the sweets and maybe even working out every now and then. You should be very proud of the steps you're taking toward a healthier you! Now I'm not here to play devil's advocate, but don't you want to enjoy the sweet things in life? I mean, hugs are great, but the occasional ice cream is too.

The ice cream truck was a quintessential part of summertime as a kid. You'd hear that tinkly wind-up-music-box tune—first in the distance, then closer as it wound its way through your neighborhood. And you'd grab your piggy bank money or change from your mom and run outside, heart pounding from panic that you'd miss out. Oh, there was nothing like an ice-cold Popsicle on a hot summer day! Even if it started melting within seconds of unwrapping and your hands got sticky right away, it was the perfect afternoon break. A visit to the ice cream truck is an oasis of sorts. That sweet afternoon treat represents calm and pure joy—no matter what else is going on in your life at the moment.

If you live in a neighborhood, hunting down your ice cream truck should be relatively easy. Keep an ear out for the classic jingle that the trucks typically play all route long. It's their calling card to let you know that they're nearby. If you're a city kidult, make a midnight run to the convenience store freezer aisle. Country kid? Head to a dairy farm or farmers' market for a midday ice cream break.

★ PRO TIP ★

You can find your local ice cream truck stops at IceCreamTrack.com. ·Cone or cup?

Change Your Identity with Role-Playing Games (RPGs)

$ $ $ | 👤👤👤👤 + 👤 | 🌳🏠

Have you ever wanted to forget everything and just get away for a little while? Even when things are going great, it's hard not to want to escape occasionally. Work overwhelms, bills and finances frustrate, and even our relationships get strained from time to time. Wouldn't it be nice if you could just leave it all behind and live another life, even for just a few hours?

Well, you totally can! The rise of RPGs allows you to assume a different identity from a different world. There are four primary types of RPGs to choose from.

First: tabletop or pen and paper RPGs. The most common one that you've probably heard of is Dungeons & Dragons. In this type there is no script and the players assume their character's personality throughout the game.

The second kind is text-based, connecting players through online forums and chats. One of the best-known text-based RPGs, OtherSpace, is accessible at JointheSAGA.com.

Live action role-playing, or LARPing, is the third type of RPG. As you might imagine, these take place in person. Players dress up as their character and play on location, where they can move around and physically interact with other players. LARPing has no script and players are free to act in character throughout the game. Find a LARPing community near you at LARPing.org.

The final type is newer in terms of RPGs and is called massively multiplayer online role-playing games (MMORPGs for short). As you can tell from the name, these are played online. Players log in and go through a series of challenges or quests to reach game goals and advance the story line. This kind is perfect for introverts.

Assuming a different identity within a game is a healthy mode of self-expression. Role-play all your worries away!

Bike It Out

We bike to work. We bike for exercise. We bike for a cause. But do we ever bike just for fun? Some of us do; others are missing out. Long bike rides during the cool evenings between May and September used to be one of the best parts of summer. Maybe we had a destination in mind, maybe not. Who cared? We had all the time in the world. Get that feeling back by getting a group of friends together and heading out on a long bike ride after work or on a Sunday morning. Feeling the wind in your hair as you cruise down Main Street to your favorite taco spot is the perfect way to end an evening or unwind before you start a new workweek. Taking a bike ride is an awesome way to burn some calories and get where you're going in a jiffy. Plus, you don't have to worry about paying for parking! Got kids? Take them with you and introduce them to the best feeling in the world.

Before heading out the door, don't forget: safety first. Make sure to wear a helmet, look both ways before crossing busy streets, and always pay attention to what is going on around you.

Find the Best Playground on the Block

Playgrounds are where imaginations truly run wild, am I right? Dashing around, ducking under slides, hanging from the monkey bars– it's where you were the king or queen of the castle or a pirate sailing the seven seas.

After overindulging on brunch, instead of lazing about for the rest of the afternoon, take out a map or do a *Google* search and find all the playgrounds within a 10-mile radius of your house. Playground equipment these days has been taken up a notch. They vary in design and even material, and chances are, you'll soon be able to figure out which playgrounds are the crown jewels of your neighborhood. (Just be sure to stick to sturdier equipment and obey any signs that say "Kids Only." Some playgrounds meant for little ones can't handle the weight of those who are adult-sized.)

Exploring playgrounds just for fun will not only bring back fun memories of your yesterdays but you'll also get the chance to play again. Spend some time hanging upside down by the monkey bars and see the world from a new perspective. Swing until you feel you could touch the sky. Breathe in some fresh air and run free!

Bonus: many parks with playgrounds will often have other fun amenities. You might find an old carousel that still works or running paths that take you through hidden forests and ponds. Let your childlike wonder lead you and have the best time ever!

MASH Up Your Future

$ $ $ | 👥 + 👨‍👩‍👧 | 🌳🏠

Do you ever find yourself dreaming about the days gone by when the possibilities were endless? Like when there was still a chance of marrying Justin Timberlake or becoming a millionaire off your start-up by age twenty. You can still dream. Just throw it back to your middle school days when you had your fortunes told by playing the game MASH.

The name of the game stands for Mansion, Apartment, Shack, House. To play, you only need a pencil, paper, and your wildest dreams. The basic version of the game has four categories: who you'll marry, the number of kids you'll have, the type of car you'll drive, and where you'll live.

To play, start by writing MASH at the top of the page. Below the heading, make three lists, each with four options: four people you want to marry (traditionally, choose two people you have a crush on, one person who would be okay to marry, and one you dislike), four cars you might own (again, two dream cars, one average car, and one terrible choice, like a garbage truck), and four numbers to represent the number of children you might have.

·FUN FOR EVERYONE·

If you've already reached the partner, house, car, and kids milestones, try other categories, such as Where I'll Retire, Next Vacation, Type of Pet, Number of Grandkids, or Midlife Crisis Splurge.

Have the player whose fortune is being told select a random number. Stick to a lower number (8 or under); otherwise you'll be counting forever. Start at the top with the letter *M* and count off until you reach the number selected. (M = 1, A = 2, and so on through the lists.) Whatever letter, word, or number you land on, scratch that off the list. Keep going until you there is only one option left in each category. Then read off the fortune.

The end of the game should go something like this: Nicole will live in an apartment, have six kids, drive a Toyota Camry, marry Dwayne Johnson, and have a vacation home in Tuscany. I can totally work with this.

Try a Paint (and Wine) Night

Swirling a paintbrush across a canvas isn't just reserved for art class. At a paint and sip party you can take a break from everyday life and indulge your creative side while relieving stress and having a few laughs. Put your own spin on classic paintings like the *Mona Lisa* or paint a self-portrait that reveals the inner you. No artistic training needed!

Method 1: Sign your gang up for a wine and paint night—they're popping up all over the place and it's easy to find one near you with a quick *Google* search. A friendly local artist will teach you some new techniques and how to re-create the image of the night in your own style.

Method 2: Organize a paint night on your own. You'll need just a few tools: paint, some paintbrushes, some canvas, and a picture for inspiration, plus some friends!

Prepare a cheese and bread plate, grab a few bottles of your favorite $5 wine, and have at it!

Mix Up Some Homemade Play-Doh

The whole act of playing with Play-Doh is a feast for the senses, from the neon-bright colors to the feel of working it with your hands, molding it into shapes, and using tools to create textures. Sitting at your kitchen table on a Sunday afternoon and getting hands-on with a big ball of Play-Doh leads to mindful, creative bliss. What? You don't have a Play-Doh set hanging around your house? No worries—this recipe for homemade Play-Doh will work just as well.

The ingredients in this homemade recipe help it last longer. It's really easy to make yourself!

YOU'LL NEED:

- 1 cup all-purpose flour, plus extra for kneading
- $1/2$ cup salt
- $3/4$–1 cup warm water
- $1^1/2$ tablespoons olive or canola oil
- 2 teaspoons cream of tartar
- Option: 3–5 drops gel food coloring

> ★ PRO TIP ★
>
> You can add an aroma-therapy element to your homemade Play-Doh by substituting brewed and cooled fruit or mint tea for the water or adding a couple drops of essential oils.

DIRECTIONS:

1. Mix together all the ingredients in a medium saucepan over medium heat. Note: start with $3/4$ cup water, adding more if needed to reach the consistency you want. Add the food coloring last. Stir gently until fully combined.
2. Remove the ball from the pan and place it on a lightly floured surface.
3. Once cool, knead until it reaches a Play Doh–like consistency.
4. If it is still sticky, add more flour 1 teaspoon at a time and continue kneading. Store your homemade Play-Doh in an airtight container so you don't find a crumbling mess later!

Throw a Frisbee

It's Saturday afternoon, you're outside at a local gem of a park you found on your playground hunt a few weeks back. The monkey bars are overrun, so what else are you to do? Play Frisbee, of course! A game of Frisbee is more than simply tossing a plastic disc back and forth. It requires a bit of skill and a keen flick of the wrist to get the Frisbee where it needs to go.

Even if you just toss the Frisbee around in your own backyard, spending some time outdoors and soaking in the sunshine will be so relaxing for your body and mind. It totally helps that you're getting some exercise in too! In fact, a Frisbee-throwing fest is a great way to exercise your pooch too. Have your dog-parent friends join you for a puppy playdate at home or a nearby park or beach and teach an old dog some fetching new tricks! (Or maybe he'll teach you.)

No pups? No problem! Challenge your friends for a bit of fun and see who can throw the Frisbee the farthest or the highest in your backyard. If it ends up in your grouchy neighbor's yard, do Rock, Paper, Scissors to determine who has to retrieve it.

Instead of just tossing a Frisbee back and forth, you can turn it into some serious competition! If you're ready for more, take your Frisbee-throwing skills to the next level with Disc Golf or Ultimate Frisbee.

Fly Through the Air

$$$ | ♟♟ + ♟♟♟ | ⚘ ⌂

Running off and joining the circus seemed like a solid plan in between language arts and science class. Who had time for all that homework anyway? In comparison, the glitz, the glam, and the entertainment of the big top were so enticing.

It's hard not to admire the talent that trapeze artists have. They somehow soar across the room with the greatest of ease, making it look completely effortless in the process. If you want to defy heights and test your timing, sign up for a trapeze lesson. Now that you're old enough to sign the waiver yourself, you can make an old dream come true!

Challenge yourself to face your fear of heights. You're going to be strapped in and there's a net below you to catch you when you fall. Take a leap of faith! (Or, go for an aerial silks class, where you can still fly and get limber, but you're just inches from the floor.) Go get 'em, tiger.

Play Ping-Pong

$ $ $ | 👫 + 👫👫 | 🌳🏠

Put your hand-eye coordination to the test when you team up with your pals to play doubles! Table tennis is a whacking good time with the right competition. Plus, knocking that ball back and forth at top speed will have you burning off all the extra calories from last night's happy hour. Take turns serving at the Ping-Pong table in your basement as you hone your skills through rapid-fire play!

Keeping track of the ball will put your mental sharpness to the test as it moves back and forth across the table at lightning speed. Even just a casual game of table tennis will make you quick on your feet. Take it up a notch and play competition style! Instead of Saturday movie nights, go all out for a game of Ping-Pong instead!

Race Go-Karts

$$$ | 👤👤 + 👤👤👤 | 🌳🏠

You have a need for speed! And it's only contained by speed limits. There's a little bit of a NASCAR driver inside all of us. You might not be able to race laps around your neighborhood, but you can on a go-kart track. Live out those race car driver fantasy dreams and go go-kart racing on Saturday afternoon.

With your adrenaline pumping, you'll be whizzing around the track, dreaming of beating out the competition and taking home that first-place trophy. Take your posse down to the track and see who has what it takes to come out on top.

Zipping around the track, accelerating through turns—you'll be a pro in no time at all when you put the pedal to the metal. Ladies and gentlemen, start your engines!

?? POP TRIVIA ??

Many professional race-tracks around the US— the ones with banked corners and sharp turns à la Mario Kart—actually allow you to bring your own car to drive around the course on what they call track day. Zoom, zoom.

Go on a Field Trip

Instead of another day dreading another nearly pointless meeting, why not take a personal day and use it to expand your mind by visiting local places of interest? Just like when you were a student, taking a field trip is a brilliant way to break up the monotony, learn some new history or information, and to make learning a priority once again. Where will your day off take you?

Bring along a few inquisitive souls and get to know what's going on in the world while taking in the sights before stopping at a new restaurant for a delicious lunch.

Best part—you don't need a permission slip and there won't be any teachers nagging you to stay with your buddy or get in line. That means you'll have to plan the field trip yourself, but that doesn't have to be complicated in the slightest. Pick a destination and use your favorite travel app to find out how to get there, what's on, and where to eat nearby. Many museums have free or low-cost admission days, so start by searching for what's available in your hometown or nearby. You can search for points of interest or local historical sites to visit and even hop on a tour if you're feeling up to it. And don't forget to submit your field trip report—on *Instagram*.

Play Slime Time, DIY Edition

It's ooey, it's gooey—it's slime time! Feeling it goop between your fingers is a sensory dream, especially for those of us who secretly want to buy a fidget spinner. Plus, it's great for little hands to shape and play with as well. Making slime at home is easy; you probably even already have the ingredients on hand!

MAKES ABOUT 1 CUP

YOU'LL NEED:

- $^1/_2$ cup thick shampoo
- $^1/_4$ cup cornstarch, or more as needed
- A few drops food coloring (color or colors of your choice)
- 5–7 tablespoons water

DIRECTIONS:

1. Mix together the shampoo and $^1/_4$ cup cornstarch in a medium bowl until combined. (Keep extra cornstarch nearby; you might need it to make your slime less sticky.)
2. Add a few drops food coloring if you want brightly colored slime. Mix and match; the colors are completely up to you.
3. Add 1 tablespoon water and continue to mix. Slowly add 4–6 more tablespoons of water, mixing until you achieve the perfect slime-like consistency: stretchy without being sticky.
4. Slime won't hold a shape. It's soft, almost silky in texture. Keep tweaking your recipe with the cornstarch and water until you achieve your desired slime. Then get squishin'!

Have a Blast with Nerf Wars

What's just as fun as paintball but far less painful? Nerf Blasters, of course! Set, aim, and fire as you get within range to tag your friends with soft foam darts. Run around your backyard and duck and cover to avoid getting hit. The Nerf Blasters of today come in cool colors and unique styles that give you a competitive edge on the road to victory. It's up to you to take out your opponents one by one and get your team a "W"!

Unlike those paintball bruises that could leave you black and blue for weeks, the foam darts of the Nerf Blasters won't hurt—as long as you avoid tagging each other in the face! Throwing a Nerf war is a family-friendly activity that's outrageously fun. Equip everyone from nieces and nephews to the grandparents at your next Fourth of July barbecue and have at it. Make it a tradition that everyone can look forward to year after year between dips in the pool and burgers.

BLAST FROM THE PAST

Nerf darts are made from neon polyurethane that was originally used for sports equipment designed specifically for indoor use. How cool!

Get Your Kicks

You kick it right between first and second and take off running! You're rounding third by the time the ball is thrown infield and just barely cross home plate in time. It's the first home run of the game! Kickball is a smashing good time for those with a competitive streak, and almost anyone can play. Round up a big group of friends and head to a big park to play on a Saturday afternoon. Better yet, make it a weekly event.

Kickball mimics baseball, in that you have a "diamond" with three bases and home plate. You can use a public baseball field at a park or even set up the bases in your backyard with bases bought at a sporting goods store. Split your squad into two teams of at least seven players each. You'll need a pitcher, a catcher, a first, second, and third baseman, and two players for the outfield. One team takes the field while the other lines up to kick the ball. This is where those elementary school soccer skills will come in handy!

There are a few ground rules to know before you play. There are four ways to be tagged out by players of the opposing team. One, if an opposing team member throws the ball and it hits you; two, if an opposing player tags you with the ball; three, if you kick the ball and the opposing team catches it before it hits the ground; and four, if an opposing player gets the ball and tags the base before you get there. After three outs, the teams switch sides and it starts over!

A run is counted when a player crosses home plate. The goal is to have the most runs after seven innings (an inning is after both teams have a chance to kick). This could go on for a while so be sure to bring some Gatorade, granola, and Cracker Jacks!

Play I Spy

$$$ | 👫 + 👪 | 🌳🏠

I spy with my little eye...something big, green, and fuzzy. Now it's up to you to sleuth out the answer! Finally, that "attention to detail" skill you put on your resume will come in handy.

This is a great game to play when you're stuck in the car or on a long plane ride. You'll have to get creative with your spy skills. If you make it too obvious, it will be too easy. The key is to pick something small that people tend to overlook instead of bigger and flashier items. Make them get out their magnifying glasses for this. Pro tip: you'll have to be witty in the way you describe the item so you don't end up giving it away too quickly!

Dip Into Oreo Cream

What is in Oreos that makes them so darn delicious? Debates have raged over whether it's the crisp chocolate cookie, the sweet cream filling, or the combination that makes this a childhood—and adult—favorite. Also: what is the best way to eat them? Dunked whole in milk or split open so you can lick the filling? And then there are Double Stuf Oreos: more of a good thing or a crime against the balanced flavors of the original? You could debate these issues for hours, or you can call a truce and create this sensational Oreo Cream Dip!

With a base made of cream cheese and marshmallow fluff, this dip makes a fabulous game night treat.

MAKES 15 SERVINGS

YOU'LL NEED:

- 8 ounces cream cheese, softened
- $^1/_4$ cup powdered sugar
- $^1/_2$ cup marshmallow fluff
- 10 Double Stuf Oreos, crumbled
- Additional Oreos, strawberries, graham crackers, or other cookies for dipping

DIRECTIONS:

1. In a large bowl, mix together the softened cream cheese and powdered sugar.
2. Once mixed, add the marshmallow fluff.
3. Fold in the crumbled Oreos. (Put the Oreos in a plastic bag and smash them for an easy way to crumble them.)
4. Transfer to a smaller bowl and serve!

Chalk It Up to Art

Get your Banksy on and decorate your sidewalks with chalk! With so many colors to choose from, there's no limit to what you can design. Brighten up your concrete with a vase of flowers or a self-portrait to make your house a unique spot on the block.

Sit down on Sunday afternoon with your bucket of sidewalk chalk and get to work. Don't let your lack of artistic ability hold you back. Dig deep into your imagination to create something truly unique. Use chalk as your medium to draw in abstract, re create famous paintings using only basic shapes, or make a nature scene in chalk pointillism. You could even draw a hopscotch court and get in a little exercise. Or take it to the next level and make some trick art to take cool *Instagram* photos with. Create your own hashtag and share it with your friends.

PART 3
YOU'RE NEVER TOO OLD FOR...

There are some things we'll just never be able to grow out of, no matter how hard we try. And truthfully, that's okay. (Though, it probably is time you start doing your laundry before you run out of underwear.) On the flip side, we have to remind ourselves that fun doesn't have an age limit. Luckily, some of your childhood favorites come in grown-up size. And they're probably even close by!

While there are plenty of things you can do to bring back the magic nostalgia of your younger years, some things just can't be easily DIYed at home. I mean, you *could* design a mini golf course or roller coaster in your backyard, but if you don't have the space or the time, it's good to know these thrills—and more—are just a ride away.

In this section of *The Kidult Handbook*, I'll reintroduce you to games, activities, and amazing locations that will really make you feel young again.

Play Mini Golf

Nailing a hole in one as you cruise across the green and laughing with friends to see who has the best shot is an excellent way to spend a Saturday afternoon. Grab a club and a golf ball and put your hand-eye coordination to the test! A game of putt-putt is a surefire way to bring out your competitive side. The player with the highest score buys a round of drinks!

Mini golf is an all-around great sport for a family or group of friends. You get to enjoy a bit of friendly competition, get in some walking, and make a few memories along the way.

If you've only experienced mini golf at the seashore, be advised they are popping up everywhere, from the suburbs to indoor venues, all over the country. Glow in the dark rounds and puppy golf are fun twists on the classic game, and you'll find fun course themes ranging from nautical to historical, monsters to astronauts. Just remember, it's okay if you're not up to par! This isn't the PGA, people.

Run an Obstacle Course

Boot camp meets *Survivor*! Scaling rope walls, crossing bridges suspended from the treetops, and zip-lining your way down—what's more fun and more challenging than an obstacle course? You'll have to use your gym-trained muscles and outdoor skills to make it through each obstacle, as they are designed to be demanding. Obstacle courses test your physical (and often mental) limits in the best way possible. Plus, done in the right spirit, they provide a fun, physical way to work out your competitive tendencies or boost team spirit.

As an adult you might have to face a few fears you didn't have as a kid, like a fear of heights. Facing these fears will give you confidence and the knowledge that you can succeed. Even if you don't make it the first time, keep trying! Each time through the course you'll get stronger and faster as you learn something new.

Getting outside, getting physical, and supporting your friends as you race across the course is exactly what you need to build camaraderie and work together to achieve a common goal. Now, who's going first?

Be Laser-Focused

Splitting into teams and chasing after your friends playing laser tag is what weekend afternoons are for! If you're a kid of the '80s, this scene will bring back memories. Separate into teams, dress in dark colors, and go! The game is on.

Laser tag takes regular tag to the next level. You'll have the best time if you head a local venue that has cool indoor variations of the game. Pro tip: don't wear white! The black lights used indoors will give your position away. These edgy laser tag spots have cool obstacles to overcome. You'll need to strategize with your teammates before the game begins to outwit your opponents. As a less intense version of paintball, laser tag is exciting for kids of all ages. Take your nieces and nephews and have at it! You'll be the coolest aunt or uncle around.

BLAST FROM THE PAST

There is a Laser Tag Museum that you can visit in Louisville, Kentucky. It opened in 2005 and it's where you'll find everything you ever wanted to know about the game. You can revisit your favorite phaser or find out what was happening in laser tag history the year you were born. Wicked.

Jump-Start a Trampoline Park

If you had a trampoline growing up, you were the luckiest kid on the block. My friends and I would spend hours jumping up and down and attempting to learn how to do backflips (front flips have always seemed to be much easier to do). There was also a game called Popcorn where one person would curl up in a ball as tightly as possible in the center of the trampoline and everyone else would bounce around as quickly as they could, trying to get the person to "pop."

While purchasing a trampoline of your own might not be the most practical thing to do at this point in your life, the good news is that there has been an upcropping of trampoline parks. These parks are indoor centers that house a huge number of connected trampolines to create endless fun. There are usually foam pits to jump into and angled trampolines to help you do cool tricks. At some you can even play games such as basketball on the trampolines. You'll finally be able to nail that slam dunk!

Jumping on a trampoline takes a lot of stamina and as such is a great way to get rid of excess energy. If you're looking for a form of exercise that will really get your heart rate up and actually be loads of fun, trampoline parks are the way to go. Grab your friends and go for an adults-only night!

Live in a Tree House

Imagine this: a cozy hideaway where you could be alone in a space all your own, above the world, inviting friends over only if you felt like it. With this space and your imagination, you could pilot a spacecraft, captain a ship, or live out your Rapunzel fantasies. What could possibly be better than that?

If you can honestly say that you never dreamed of having a tree house, I wouldn't believe you. I would bet that a tree house is the most desired kid dream of all time. Even if you had your own room at home, a tree house still brings with it a degree of privacy that, as a kid, was empowering. As an adult, well, that privacy is great for other things.

Luckily, you no longer have to scour your backyard for the perfect tree and beg your parents to haul out the tools and lumber. Tree house hotels are on the rise (hah!) and are popping up as popular destinations all around the globe.

From the forests of Washington State to the shores of California to the outskirts of Brighton, England, and around the world, these engineering feats are suspended off the ground with amenities you wouldn't possibly have dreamed of as a seven-year-old. They often come with hot tubs, decks, room service, and of course, an unbeatable view with the privacy you crave.

Reach Playground Level: Adult

Ten-story slides, swings that light up at night, carousels made of sea glass—and all for us kidults. Adult-sized and -themed playgrounds and playground equipment can be found in many major cities around the world. Some are more extreme than others, but all offer kid-style fun with an adult attitude.

You'll have to search a bit more to find an adult playground, but it's worth it. There are various types of these hot spots all around the world. From skate parks to rock climbing centers to unique structures such as MountMitte, a massive high-wire course in Berlin, Germany, these locations take playgrounds to the next level.

If you're more comfortable at Level 1, monkey bars, swings, and ball pits abound at these specialty spots made just for people who never outgrew recess.

In fact, taking a recess break is a great way to clear your mind and get some fresh air and exercise. Find an adult playground—or even a park with a fitness course, and spend an hour zooming from one piece of equipment to another. See if you can make your way across the monkey bars without falling. See, all of those sessions at the gym are paying off. I call first on the swings!

Splash in a Water Park

What's better than relaxing the day away floating around a lazy river? I know—floating around the lazy river with a cocktail in hand. As a kid, the lazy river is the most boring part of a water park. But as an adult? It's relaxation central.

If cocktail lounging is not quite your speed, check out the other activities at water parks. They usually have something for everyone, from the stress-free lazy river and family-friendly kiddie pools to intricate mazes of unique water features and high-octane water slides.

Take the family or gather some friends and go explore! Spending the day at a water park is a fun way to bond with your tribe, cool off in the summer heat, and get a healthy dose of vitamin D.

Use this as a time to get out of your comfort zone. Challenge yourself to go down the tallest slide at the park or be the first of your group to suggest going on the newest attraction. Bonus points if you convince everyone in your group to go with you. Don't forget the towels and sunscreen!

Visit an Aquarium

$$$ | 👥+👥👥 | 🌳🏠

Do you know why doctors' and dentists' waiting rooms often have fish tanks? Because gazing at fish gliding around in the water reduces blood pressure and heart rate. So, when you're feeling stressed and want to relax, head to the aquarium! Watching sharks, octopuses, plankton, and jellyfish swim by in hypnotic rhythm is not only relaxing, it's also a brilliant way to spend a rainy day when you can't be outdoors. Wandering through an underwater world will keep you intrigued as you take in the beautiful and diverse ecosystems that thrive in our oceans.

At the aquarium you can touch a starfish, see the creatures that live in the darkest depths of our planet's waters, and be amazed by how much we still have to uncover about them. Many locations have specialty seminars hosted by experts where you can learn more and even ask questions. Take your kids or even your parents and encourage everyone to take part in this special opportunity. The aquarium is a great place for a date, too, but feel free to go there on your own. You could learn the difference between a lagoon and a fjord or get the basics of bioluminescence. The world is your oyster!

Plan Your Escape

Imagine an evil scientist has locked you and a bunch of strangers in a room and set a timer. If you and your fellow prisoners don't solve the clues he's set for you by the time it goes off, the room will explode. Will you panic? Or will you enjoy the thrill of living out your favorite board game mysteries and suspense thriller scenarios as you race against the clock? In an Escape Room game, you get to find out.

Not only are these events fun and exciting, but they also promote teamwork and critical thinking by placing you in a situation where your full concentration is on the tasks at hand. (Tip: it wouldn't hurt to have someone with Hermione Granger–like skills on your team to help you puzzle out the solutions.)

Escape Room venues and amusement centers have popped up all over. Search for an Escape Room near you, round up your squad, and make a reservation. Or, plunder the Internet for ideas on how to create your own. Either way, adventure is waiting, Indiana Jones.

Get a Ticket to Ride

$$$ | 2 + 3 people | outdoor / indoor

Whose heart doesn't start racing at the sight of a lit-up neon Ferris wheel and the scents of popcorn and cotton candy? Remember when you would drive past a pop-up amusement park or state fair and beg your parents to take you? Now you can go anytime you want, buy all the ride tickets you want, and keep trying for that stuffed bear until you win it. Ride the bumper cars and the flying swings, chomp a candy apple, and show your partner you got game down the strip.

Of course, if you really want to ride on the wild side, you'll head for the roller coaster. The anticipation as you lurch to the top of the highest hill of the park is nothing compared to the adrenaline that pumps through your body on your way down. Zoom through loop-de-loops, over gravity-defying turns, and down gut-wrenching drops. Not all roller coasters are quite so intense, though. You can always opt for a wooden roller coaster if that's more your style. You'll probably find a smoother ride with the newest beasts of engineering, though, as the ride is far less choppy.

POP TRIVIA

The oldest operating wooden roller coaster in the US is located in Lakemont Park in Altoona, Pennsylvania. It was built in 1902!

Visit a Petting Zoo

Animals have a calming influence on us—it's true! From pigs to puppies to lizards, spending time with members of the animal kingdom has been shown to reduce stress and even blood pressure. Now that's something we could all take advantage of! So, what could be better than spending an afternoon cuddling cute animal friends? Who can possibly resist petting a wooly sheep or feeding some fluffy ducklings?

It's pretty easy to find a petting zoo, especially in the summer and fall when there are fairs and farms open for berry and apple picking. City and suburban zoos usually have them, too, and you don't even have to borrow a kid to get in! But there are other ways to experience the joy of animals. Cute and quirky cat cafés have opened in many cities around the world where you can enjoy the company of these felines while sipping your latte (some places even double as cat adoption centers). There are also mobile petting zoos that will bring the animals straight to your office. Watch out everybody—Bessie the pig is running down the hallway. And if those aren't easily accessible to you, go play with your friend's new puppy or volunteer to cat sit the next time your neighbor is out of town. It's good for you!

Go on a Treasure Hunt

Reading the clues and searching for the treasure puts your mind to work. You'll have to read between the lines, interpret the map, and outwit the others to beat them to the treasure. Luckily, you probably won't run into pirates as you search for the gold!

Round up a group of friends and set out on a premade treasure hunt through an app or website or find a local spot that will set up one for you for a fee. Treasure hunts and scavenger hunts are back in vogue and new variations are popping up all the time.

To DIY your own, make a list of items, within a household or city-wide, and run a photo scavenger hunt. Each player or team will have to take a photo of every item on the list. The first team to successfully do so wins.

PART 4
PARTY, PARTY, PARTY

Everyone loves a good party. As long as there are tasty snacks available and quality entertainment on deck, even the introverts among us will have a smashing good time. Sure, we throw parties for birthdays and holidays, but when was the last time you threw a bash just for the fun of it? Can I let you in on a secret? No one ever needed a reason to throw a party! They're the perfect excuse to get loose and eat a little extra dessert or enjoy an adult beverage.

But I'm not talking about fussy—and boring—parties where you have to act like a grownup and make small talk, or lazy ones where you binge-watch TV together. No, the party games and activities here will have you giggling, getting up on your feet, and getting to know one another better than ever (or for the first time). So organize your living room, turn on some tunes to set the mood, pull out your favorite games from childhood (or invent some new ones to keep everyone on their toes), and set out the snack trays—let's get this party started! I've got your next kidult shindig covered. You'll be the best hostess around, promise.

Get Twisted

Getting twisty with your friends will lead to laughs all around! Dig out that old game of Twister you have hidden in the back of your closet and see how flexible you really are. (Yogis have an advantage here.) Have one player spin the Twister wheel for everyone playing the game. The other players will then go through the motions of left foot red, right hand blue, right foot green, and so on, until there's only one player left standing. The one with the best balance wins!

Turn your casual game of Twister into a rapid pace, competition-style elimination game. Spin the wheel every 10 seconds, giving players minimal time to contort their bodies around the game board. The quicker the pace, the better. The player who makes it through without falling over is the official Twister Champion.

Play Sticker Stalker

Sticker Stalker is a sneaky game that's a fun addition to any shindig you throw. Not only does it bring out your sly, snickering inner child, but it's a great icebreaker for corporate meetings and other gatherings where you want people to get to know one another in a hurry without an overdose of awkwardness. It's also perfect for introverts who can use their powers of invisibility to stick it to others.

The rules are simple: get rid of all your stickers by sticking them on guests at the party without anyone noticing. And if you get caught? Your sticker is returned to you and the person who catches you then gets to put one of his stickers on you. The first person to get rid of all her stickers wins the game.

Sounds easy enough, right? I hate to burst your bubble, but the old "patting your friend on the back" trick will work maybe once throughout the game (and that's if you're really lucky). Be prepared to get creative with your moves to get rid of those stickers.

To keep track of who puts their stickers where, have different colors or types of stickers for each guest. Make it extra festive and match the stickers to your party theme. Limit the number of stickers per person to around five to ten so the game doesn't go on too long.

Want more of a challenge? Set a time limit or add the rule that each of your stickers has to go on a different person. May the stealthiest friend win.

FUN FOR EVERYONE

For a fun twist, match the sticker theme to cartoon characters of your youth!

Pin the Tail on the Donkey

$ $ $ | 👤👤👤👤 + 👤 | 🌳 🏠

Your eyes are covered, and then a friend takes you by the shoulders, turns you around a few times, and points you in the right direction as you stumble forward with your hands out searching for something solid—preferably the wall with the picture of the donkey on it! Pinning the tail on the donkey is not as easy as it sounds. Losing your vision, even for a moment, forces you to rely on your other senses to complete the task. The real challenge is getting the tail near the donkey's rear—you'll have to feel it out to make it happen! Of course, part of the fun is watching other people pin the tail in the wrong place.

The first thing to do is to mount the tail-less donkey on the wall. All the partygoers get a tail with a tack or tape that they write their name on to keep track of who pinned what where. Phew. Players are then blindfolded and spun around five times, pointed in the direction of the donkey, and sent forth on their own like teenagers into adulthood.

The more disoriented the players are, the funnier the outcomes will be! Try playing this after everyone's had a cocktail or two. First person to toss his drink loses.

FUN FOR EVERYONE

Change the "donkey" to another animal or character to fit your party theme, or just choose something fun! For example, pin the head on the birthday boy or girl, or pin the heart on the '90s boy band members or '70s rock band members.

74

Play *The Newlywed Game*—
Friends Edition

How much do you *really* know about your BFFs? Find out when you play *The Newlywed Game*—friends edition! When you're with a close group of friends, it's fun to reminisce on all the memories you've made together over the years. (You remember the game, right? Where newly married couples try to match answers to questions about each other's likes, dislikes, and habits? This version's for old—and not so old—friends.)

Cozy up around a fireplace or the pool and pair up to see how well you've paid attention to the details of your friends' lives. You can play *The Newlywed Game* as individuals or on teams. Basic questions range from what's your friend's favorite color, food, or vacation destination to things like which restaurant you went to for your first dinner together or who texted who first. Choose questions based on your unique friendships or do a simple *Google* search to find a set of predetermined questions that fit the bill.

Asking questions about each other helps you get back to the basics of your relationships and reconnect on an intimate level that gets lost in your busy lives. When it's game over, you'll have new memories from this party to bring up in your next game!

Play Musical Chairs

"Bumbumbum dum bum screeeeech." When the music stops, don't be the only person left standing or you're out! Musical Chairs is easy—all you need is as many chairs as you have players, minus one (i.e., if you have ten people, you need nine chairs), your phone to play some tunes, and a volunteer to play the music.

Put the chairs in a circle or back to back (in this example, five chairs will be back to back with four chairs). When the music starts, the players walk single file in one direction around the grouped chairs. As long as the music is playing, keep moving. At random, the volunteer stops the music and everyone finds a chair as soon as possible and plants their butt in it. If you're still standing, you're out of the game.

Remove one of the chairs and start the music again. As a player is eliminated, so is a chair. The game gets more difficult as the players dwindle down. Last player sitting wins.

It's all fun and games to get yourself in a chair, especially if two people try to sit on the same chair at once! Just don't be the person shoving other players out of the way—you'll want to get to your chair fair and square.

Tell Two Truths (and a Lie)

You were taught to tell the truth, the whole truth, and nothing but the truth, so...how well can you tell a lie? This game is part deception, part detection, and part using the old thinking cap.

This game is played just as you'd suspect: each player shares three pieces of information about herself. Two of them are true and the other is false. It's up to the other players of the game to determine which piece of information is the lie. Bring your magnifying glass; you'll be sniffing around for clues!

One winning tactic is to use truths that seem like lies because they are hard to believe. Up until I was twenty-one, when I flew in an airplane for the first time, I always included, "I've never been on an airplane" as one of my truths. For many people, especially college-aged individuals, this was hard to buy as the truth. Those are the types of facts you'll want to use to trick the other players.

And what's the best way to detect the lies? Look for telling body language, facts that seem so hard to believe that maybe they're true after all (see "winning" tip in previous paragraph), and the player's inflection—is he "selling" a fact as an obvious truth or lie?

If all else fails, keep in mind that the best lies are the ones that are mostly true. To keep your pals on their toes, change one slight fact about the lie that you give—it will make the game more challenging for everyone involved! Like *The Newlywed Game*, you'll learn new things about your friends, making those relationships even stronger!

Revive Charades

In a world where we mostly communicate electronically and use emojis to convey nuance and meaning, Charades gives you a chance to use non-verbal body language and ingenuity to get the message across. It's fun to play both with people you know and people you don't know. As the game goes on, you'll get better and better.

To play, you could print a random list of prompts from online, or have each person contribute a few ideas to the pile for the opposing team (this is so it's not easy for you to guess your own charade when it's being acted out by your teammate).

Families tend to pass down their own set of rules for this game, so make sure your group agrees on the symbols used for "book," "movie," etc. and how to signify a phrase, the number of words, number of syllables, etc. If necessary, consult the Internet for how-to tips.

Charades is a versatile game and can be played with a group of friends, on a corporate retreat, or even as an exercise to teach lessons or illustrate principles in a classroom or work environment. Get creative, but don't use your words!

J-J-J-Jenga!

$$$ | 👫+👫👤 | 🌳🏠

Remove a block without toppling the tower and you survive another round in this stacking game! It takes skill to determine which blocks of the tower aren't structural and can be removed with ease. You'll have to have a keen eye for strategizing your next move and the dexterity to pull it off. But be quick! The official game rules give players only 10 seconds before their turn ends.

Don't be the one who knocks the tower over or you end the game! In Jenga, the winner of the game is determined as the last person who successfully moved a block from within the tower and placed it on top. For this game, it's not about winning; it's about not losing. That means you'll want to pay close attention to what the other players are doing before making your move.

A game of Jenga is usually quick, lasting around 15 minutes at most. You can really play with any number of players, making it a choice party game. And it takes only a minute or two to restack the blocks, so continued game play is no problem at all. Find a local bar near you that offers Jenga XL on game night.

Take a Chance with Truth or Dare?

$$\$ \$ \$ \mid \text{👤👤👤👤} + \text{👤} \mid \text{🌳🏠}$$

Spill your guts, or do something embarrassing? The stakes are high in this game! Truth or Dare—that favorite of middle school slumber parties and college confessionals—keeps you on the edge of your seat as you go around the room just waiting for who's going to ask what and how far you'll go.

This either-or game pushes you out of your comfort zone and into the frying pan with dares that could range from eating a habanero pepper to cannonballing into the pool with your clothes on. If you think you're going to play it safe with truth, think again! Truths can be just as sticky as dares when you're asked what you really think of your girlfriend's hair. You'll definitely end up with some riotous moments by the end of the night if you really bring the creativity. Just promise us you won't do anything truly dangerous or illegal, okay?

Other than that, it's really up to you whether calamity—or hilarity—will ensue. So what will it be? Truth...or dare?

Go Pajama Streaking

Although streaking (you know, running outside *naked*) is probably out of the question for most of us who live in well-lit neighborhoods (for your sake and mine), pajama streaking is something that's almost just as fun.

Pajama streaking is running around your neighborhood in your pajamas. As kids this might involve grabbing a flashlight and sneaking out in the middle of the night with your friends. You'd run through your backyard or down your street in just your PJs, looping around the block before anyone saw you.

Obviously, this is even funnier when a bunch of so-called adults does it. So, next time your friends are over, have them bring their pajamas. Or, pass out a bunch of animal onesies when they arrive. Then when all is dark and quiet outside, make a run for it. If jogging down the street in your almost-underwear isn't your thing, pile everyone into your car and go to the nearest drive-through for ice cream or fries.

You'll feel a little rebellious going out in your pajamas (don't tell your grandma!) and having fun with your gals. What happens at girls' night, stays at girls' night—I'll never tell.

Play Quidditch Pong

Beer pong and the golden snitch collide in the riveting game of Quidditch Pong. Bring the fictional Harry Potter game you've always wished you could play to life with a few materials and a little imagination.

Beer pong is played with ten cups on each side of the table arranged in a 1-2-3-4 formation. To match the party theme, make three Quidditch goal posts of various sizes using dowel rods and tubing or embroidery hoops from a craft shop. Paint your Ping-Pong ball gold to be the golden snitch—it takes the game to a whole new level!

Pick your house—Gryffindor, Slytherin, etc.—and the blow the whistle. It's game time! You get one point for each shot you land in a cup. You get two points for each shot that goes through a goal and lands in a cup. Don't forget to fill your cups with (butter)beer and drink every time you land a shot. Make Madam Hooch proud.

FUN FOR EVERYONE:
Use water or nonalcoholic ginger beer instead of beer to make the game appropriate for all ages.

Play Fruit Basket

This fast-paced mix-and-match game (a variation on musical chairs) will keep you on your toes as you scramble not to be the odd one out.

To play, separate all the players into equal teams (for a small group of twelve people, you might have three teams with four people; for a large group with twenty or more people, you might have five teams with four people each). Each team will be something different. For example, traditionally the teams are named for different fruits (hence the name of the game), but you could use vice presidents, stores at the mall, colors, states, countries, parts of a cell, etc. You really get to flex your creative muscles with this one! Have all the players form a large circle making sure no one is standing (or sitting, if you prefer) next to a member of their own team. One player either volunteers or is selected to stand in the middle of the circle. When the game begins, the player in the center calls out a team name. All the members of that team and the player in the middle then scramble around to move to a new spot as quickly as possible. Whoever is left without a spot is now in the middle and it's that person's turn to call a new team name. At random, the player in the middle may call out "Fruit basket!" (or "Rainbow" for color teams or "United States" for state teams), and then everyone must scramble around at once to find a new place. This works best if players are seated, but either way, hilarity will most likely ensue.

Fruit Basket makes an entertaining after-dinner activity when you have a large crowd, such as at Friendsgiving or a Christmas party. In fact, the more players, the more fun you'll have.

Be a Supreme Overlord
(aka Simon Says...)

Whatever Simon says, goes! Yes, you last played this game when you were six, but now you're much more likely to relish making your adult buddies do silly things at your whim. And it is way trickier now to get them to slip up and obey you without saying "Simon Says."

To review: one person gets to be Simon, aka the boss, who then tells the other players to do various things like touch their toes or rub their nose. The catch is the players should only do the actions that are preceded by the phrase "Simon Says." If Simon doesn't say and you do it anyway, you're out of the game. It goes on until there is only one player left and a winner is declared, who then becomes the next Simon.

Play rapid-fire games of Simon Says in quick succession to see who has the best ear for direction. The better you know your players, the more outrageous and silly the commands can be. Scratch your elbow. Wait, Simon didn't say...

Explore with Marco Polo

Put yourself to the test at your next pool party with a thrilling game of Marco Polo. You'll be splashing around the pool trying to find your friends as they shout back "Polo" to your "Marco." Have everyone use funny voices to make it even more challenging as you navigate your way around unicorn- and pizza-shaped floats.

The idea behind Marco Polo is that you're playing tag but without your vision. You have to rely on only your ears to tag the other players and win the game. Start by tying a scarf around your eyes as the other players scatter throughout the pool. The game starts when you say "Marco." The other players must respond with "Polo" to help you locate them. Not replying is forfeiting the game, and that's no fun! Chase your pals around the pool as you try to catch them.

You can also play Marco Polo without a pool—your backyard will do. And the same rules apply. This is a great game for grandparents to play with young grandkids too.

Whack a Piñata

$$$ | 👤👤👤+👤 | 🌳🏠

Nothing says a party like a piñata! You'll take turns whacking at the object suspended in the air, just waiting to see who will burst it open and send all the candy flying. You can buy piñatas in all shapes and motifs, but it's more fun to make your own piñata to match your party theme using the papier-mâché method!

To DIY your own piñata, you'll need to create your desired shape. Depending on the shape you want, you will use a combination of balloons and cardboard. Use cardboard for the parts of the design that will not be holding candy. A balloon works best for the part of the piñata that will hold the goodies.

To papier-mâché the balloon elements, start by tearing up pieces of newspaper. Mix together $3/4$ cup white craft glue and $1/4$ cup water. Dip the pieces of newspaper into the glue mixture, getting them wet but not soaking—you may need to squeeze off the excess. Begin draping them over the balloon. You'll want to cover the entire balloon in three to four layers of papier-mâché.

Leave the piñata to dry overnight; it may take as long as 48 hours to dry completely. Once dry, cut a trap door into the papier-mâché. Use a craft knife to cut into the papier-mâché until you hit the balloon. Pop it with the edge of the knife and continue to make your way around, completing three sides of a square, making a flap to insert the candy.

Now it's time to finish decorating your piñata. Use paint, fabric, cardboard, feathers, or anything else you need. Let dry, then load it up with candy and seal the trap door with tape. Hint: instead of—or in addition to—candy, consider adding scratch tickets, mini bottles of alcohol (plastic, if you can find them), lip balms, temporary tattoos, small toys that match your theme, dollar bills, and so on. Hang up your piñata (outside, if possible). And take a tip from those "Fail" videos on *YouTube*: use a plastic (rather than wood or metal) bat to hit the piñata and make sure everyone else stands *way* back while it's being wielded.

Host a Sleepover Girls' Night In

Instead of the monthly girls' night out, get your squad together for one massive sleepover. Find some classics to stream like *Clueless* or *Mean Girls*. Have everyone bring their coziest pajamas and their skin care regimen—hey, those nightly serums and moisturizers are important for keeping our skin healthy and glowing. Pass out face masks and take pics!

Sleepovers at your best friend's house were part of the quintessential grade school experience. Fun nights spent catching up with friends, trading secrets, sharing dreams, playing Truth or Dare—those were important bonding experiences that we need now more than ever.

Any of the snacks in this book would be welcome at a sleepover, but since this is girls' night in, pizza should probably be on the menu. And if everyone is ready to pass out before 10 p.m.? Well there's no shame in that, you early bird. Just make sure no one tries to pierce your ears while you sleep!

Lights! Camera! Outdoor Movie Night!

Host a pop-up drive-in for your friends or everyone in your neighborhood. Invite everyone over and tell them to bring their own snacks and drinks. Not only will it be a great bonding experience, but you'll be the coolest house in the neighborhood!

Sitting outside under the stars and watching your favorite movie of all time is a great way to relax at the end of a long week. Reminiscent of a night at the drive-in, hosting an outdoor movie night is a fun way to bring back that blast from the past. It doesn't have to be complicated either.

A projector is a great way to play a movie on the side of your house. There are mini USB projectors available for under $100 that are made just for this purpose. You could also haul your TV outside, or even just use your laptop to stream a movie as you and your friends lay out blankets, pop some popcorn, and relax!

Have a Picnic Party

When was the last time you had a picnic? Not the fancy gourmet-basket kind with wine and real china. The kind where you sit on a blanket on a calm, clear day and lazily enjoy the sunshine while you eat sandwiches.

Organizing a picnic for you and your friends to enjoy should be a breeze. All you really need to do is pick a place and time, call your friends, grab a blanket, and bring snacks. Pick a clear spot away from water, animals, and potential hazards, though. You wouldn't want your picnic to end with ants in your pants or a swarm of swans attacking. That's a dance nobody wants to do!

Go all out and give your picnic a theme, like a school lunch picnic party. Drawing inspiration back from your school lunch days, what meals were go-tos for you and your friend group? PB and J? Ham and cheese? Bagels? Chocolate milk or apple juice? Have everyone bring their favorite snack or meal from grade school. Sharing is caring, so it would be fun if everyone brought their favorite school snacks and reminisced. Don't forget the bug spray and sunscreen if you're heading out during the summer months. And how about a game of freeze tag after lunch?

Apparate to a Harry Potter Party

If you were in middle school when *Harry Potter and the Sorcerer's Stone* came out, chances are it defined your childhood. As students of Hogwarts, we've all sorted ourselves into our houses, dreamt of playing Quidditch, and wished we were worried about Potions class or Defense Against the Dark Arts rather than social studies or French. Although most of us probably had a Harry Potter–themed birthday party—or at least went to one—there's no reason why the magic has to end. Bring Hogwarts to life by hosting your own Harry Potter party!

Have all your partygoers come dressed in their house colors: scarlet (or red) and gold for Gryffindor, green and silver for Slytherin, blue and bronze for Ravenclaw, and yellow and black for Hufflepuff. If you're feeling extremely festive, decorate your space to match the decor from the books. Set up a Platform Nine and Three-Quarters, Dumbledore's office, or the Great Hall as a photo booth backdrop for *Instagram* pics! And don't forget the Potions lab (aka "bar").

You can serve all types of wizarding world-related snacks, such as chocolate frogs or Harry Potter Bertie Bott's Every Flavour Beans. Split up into houses and play Quidditch Pong (a combination of Quidditch and beer pong). For a low-key evening, make the Butterbeer Milkshake recipe in this chapter and watch a movie or two. *Accio*, remote!

Host an Everybody Into the Pool Party

Splish, splash—you're having a blast! Swimming the afternoon away as you dive underwater, play pool volleyball, or float on a pool noodle is a great way to relieve stress and soak up the rays. Gather the squad and hang out at the pool while hosting a barbecue to beat out the summer heat.

Whip up some light and fresh meals, such as a summer salad, caprese skewers, and grilled chicken. Your guests can serve themselves as they alternate between taking a dip and sunbathing. Take a break from the heat and go inside for a game of Twister or Jenga! If you don't have a pool, a Slip 'N Slide or a sprinkler makes for great water activities as well. Freeze the ice pops and prepare the frosé—your poppin' pool party is underway!

FUN FOR EVERYONE

Throw it back *Gidget Goes Hawaiian* style by giving your pool party a '60s luau theme, complete with leis, ham and pineapple kebobs, Elvis or Don Ho on the record player, and Hawaiian shirts for guys and tropical print beach sarongs for the gals. Or, take it to the '90s with a (little) mermaid theme.

Take Time for Tea

$$$ | ♀♀ + ♀♀♀ | 🌳 🏠

Sipping tea out of the finest of china dressed in your Sunday best is a darling way to spend a weekend afternoon. Invite your girlfriends over and serve afternoon tea as everyone dresses the part and catches up over pastries and finger sandwiches.

Setting the stage is as easy as borrowing some doilies from your grandma, putting out a selection of tea (go with Earl Grey, Assam, or Darjeeling for an authentic assortment), a few pastries and savory dishes, and the teacups you keep hidden in the back of your storage closet. (No china teacups? Ask your gran or hit the thrift shop—it's fine if they don't match!) Tell your guests to dress fancy (extra points for wearing hats) and you're basically royalty. Okay—maybe not, but we can totally pretend, right?

Set out milk, lemon, and sugar for your guests to add to their tea. Serve your tea between four and six in the afternoon if you're going for classic afternoon tea. Or, turn your tea party into a garden party that everyone can enjoy!

?? POP TRIVIA ??

Afternoon tea and high tea are not the same. Afternoon tea is the fancy version served at hotels and tearooms, featuring scones, cakes, and dainty sandwiches. High tea is a hot, filling meal traditionally served after work at a high table (such as a kitchen table)—more like what Americans would call "supper."

Freeze Gourmet Ice Pops

There's nothing quite like an icy Popsicle on a hot summer's day. The basic DIY recipe is quite simple and you can easily customize them to your own personal taste with fruit, candy, yogurt, juice, or—for adults—a little alcohol! You'll need a 6-piece ice pop mold for this recipe. Or, you can use paper cups and wooden ice pop sticks.

MAKES 6 SERVINGS

YOU'LL NEED:

- 2 cups liquid base of your choice: water, coconut milk or coconut water, almond milk, soy milk, aloe water, or any type of fruit juice (apple, cranberry, etc.); if you want to use booze, pair the type of alcohol with a complementary liquid base (e.g., coconut milk with rum, fruity bourbon with lemonade)
- 1 cup frozen fruit of your choice

DIRECTIONS:

1. Add the liquid base and frozen fruit to a blender and blend well.
2. Pour equal amounts of the mixture into each mold.
3. Put the pops in the freezer for a minimum of 3 hours or until frozen solid.
4. To remove the ice pops from the molds, run the molds under warm water (or dip in a bowl of warm water) 15–20 seconds.

If you need some flavor inspiration, here are combinations I recommend trying:

- Blueberry and lemon in vanilla yogurt
- Cucumber, blackberry, and strawberry in coconut water
- Watermelon and lime in coconut water

Make Adult Slushies—aka Frosé

Frosé has less sugar in it than a store-bought slushie and it's lighter than a typical cocktail. There's even real fruit involved, so it's as healthy as one can get when there's wine involved!

MAKES 4 SERVINGS

YOU'LL NEED:

- 1 (750 ml) bottle rosé wine
- $^1/_2$ cup water
- $^1/_4$ cup granulated sugar
- 4 ounces strawberries, chopped
- 4 ounces raspberries or blackberries, chopped
- 5 tablespoons lemon juice

DIRECTIONS:

1. Put the rosé in the freezer for at least 6 hours. Overnight is preferred.
2. Make a simple syrup by mixing the water and sugar in a large saucepan over medium heat. Stir until the sugar has dissolved and the liquid is completely clear. Let cool completely before the next step.
3. Add the strawberries and raspberries. Note: if you have time, put the syrup with the chopped fruit in the refrigerator overnight. This will allow the flavor of the fruit to be infused into the syrup. This step isn't necessary but does create a richer flavor profile.
4. Optional: before you blend the simple syrup, pour it through a colander or cheesecloth to remove the fruit. If you skip this step and keep the fruit in the simple syrup, the final product will have an icier consistency.
5. When your rosé is done freezing and your syrup is done infusing, remove them from the freezer and put them in a blender. Add the lemon juice and blend to the desired consistency.
6. Return the frosé to the freezer for a minimum of 30 minutes.

Pop Some Rosemary Kettle Corn

A little savory, a little salty—Rosemary Kettle Corn is just the air of sophistication you're looking for to add to your sleepover party!

You'll be surprised at how easy it is to make too. If you want something a little gourmet to pair with your chardonnay, this will quickly become your go-to recipe.

Tip: have all your ingredients ready to go ahead of time—everything happens quickly!

MAKES 2–4 SERVINGS (ABOUT 8 CUPS POPPED)

YOU'LL NEED:

- ¼ cup olive oil
- 3 tablespoons granulated sugar
- 1–1½ teaspoons kosher salt, divided
- ½ cup popcorn kernels
- 2 teaspoons dried rosemary

DIRECTIONS:

1. Begin by heating the oil, sugar, and ½ teaspoon kosher salt over medium heat in a 6–8-quart pot with a glass lid.
2. Add a few popcorn kernels to the pot. Cover with the lid. (These are your tester kernels. Once they pop, you know the oil is ready.)
3. When the kernels begin popping, add the remaining popcorn kernels to the pot.
4. Place the lid on the pot and watch closely as the kernels begin popping. Lift the pot by both handles and shake gently to ensure all kernels are popping evenly.
5. Once all kernels have popped, quickly remove from heat and stir in the rosemary and optional additional salt to taste using a wooden spoon.
6. Serve and eat immediately.

Snap, Crackle, Pop 'em in Your Mouth

$$\$\,\$\,\$$ | 👤👤👤👤👤+ | 🌳🏠

Rice Krispies Treats are one of those sweet and delicious childhood pleasures that are just plain fun to eat. And now that you can cook for yourself, you can have them anytime! Pro tip: pack them in plastic wrap or parchment paper and pack one in your lunch.

MAKES 16 SERVINGS

YOU'LL NEED:

- $1/4$ cup butter
- 5 cups mini marshmallows
- 6 cups Rice Krispies cereal

Optional:

- $1\,1/2$ cups chocolate chips
- 1 teaspoon sea salt

BLAST FROM THE PAST

The Rice Krispies characters Snap, Crackle, and Pop have had several makeovers since they debuted in 1941. Over the years their cheeks have become more (and then less) rosy, their clothing has become more colorful, and in the twenty-first century they took on a digital look.

DIRECTIONS:

1. Melt the butter in a large saucepan over medium-low heat. Stir gently to keep the butter from burning.
2. Slowly add the marshmallows, stirring until they melt and mix with the butter. When melted, remove from heat.
3. Line an 8" × 8" baking pan with wax paper.
4. Add the cereal to the pan. Pour the melted butter and marshmallow mixture over the top. Use a spatula to mix the ingredients, and then spread out the mixture in an even layer on the bottom of the pan.
5. Optional: melt the chocolate chips with the sea salt over medium-low heat, stirring regularly to prevent the chocolate from burning. Pour the melted chocolate over the treats.
6. Allow the treats to set and cool about 1–2 hours.

Get Tipsy with Adult Gummy Bears

$ $$ | ♟♟♟♟♟+ | 🌳 🏠

These gummy bears are a fruity treat leveled up with the addition of your favorite alcohol. Gummy bears that get you tipsy? Sign me up!

While these might be considered a version of Jell-O shots, this recipe is much simpler and requires just two ingredients and a little bit of time. Not to mention it's easily scalable for any size party you're throwing.

MAKES 12 SERVINGS

YOU'LL NEED:

- 1 (5-ounce) bag gummy bears
- 1½ cups alcohol of your choice, or as needed (lighter alcohols work better for this recipe—think along the lines of vodka, tequila, or rum)

DIRECTIONS:

1. Empty the gummy bears into a medium bowl.
2. Pour the alcohol over the gummy bears until covered.
3. Put the bowl in the refrigerator and let sit at least 1 hour or preferably overnight. This allows the gummy bears to absorb the alcohol.
4. Use a slotted spoon to remove the gummy bears or use a colander to strain out the remaining alcohol before serving. Drink or discard any leftover alcohol.

Make a Sweet Sandwich: Peanut Butter, Honey, and Banana

$ $ $ | 👤👤👤👤👤+ | 🌳🏠

Peanut butter, honey, and banana sandwiches are one of the simplest and easiest treats to make. The honey adds a hint of sweetness to the classic combination of peanut butter and banana. It gives you your sweet-salty fix and it's relatively healthy too—especially if you choose a whole-grain bread. Bring these to your school picnic lunch party!

MAKES 1 SERVING

YOU'LL NEED:

- 2 slices bread (type of your choice)
- 1 tablespoon peanut butter, divided
- 2 teaspoons honey, divided
- $\frac{1}{2}$ medium banana, sliced

DIRECTIONS:

1. Place the bread on a work surface.
2. Spread $\frac{1}{2}$ tablespoon peanut butter on each piece of bread.
3. Drizzle 1 teaspoon honey on each piece of bread.
4. Place the banana pieces in rows of three on top of the honey on one piece of bread.
5. Take the second piece of bread and lay it (peanut butter and honey side down) on top of the banana.
6. Slice into triangles or squares and enjoy!

Munch Some Cucumber Sandwiches

Finger sandwiches make the best party food. They're cute, easy to pass around, and easy to make! Serve these up at your next tea party if you're feeling fancy.

MAKES 2 SERVINGS

YOU'LL NEED:

- 1 tablespoon cream cheese
- 2 pieces bread (type of your choice)
- Lemon zest to taste
- 1 cucumber, peeled and evenly sliced (look for English cucumbers; they have fewer seeds)

DIRECTIONS:

1. Spread the cream cheese on one slice of bread.
2. Sprinkle the lemon zest over the cream cheese. (When zesting lemon rind, be sure to just use the yellow part of the lemon, not the white pith, which is bitter.)
3. Place the cucumber slices on top of the cream cheese.
4. Place the remaining piece of bread on top of the cucumbers. Slice off the crusts, cut into triangles, and serve.

Haul to Hogsmeade for a Butterbeer Milkshake

Actually, you don't have to be a wizard to make this treat. Butterbeer, the fictional libation from the world of Harry Potter, has been brought to life in the muggle world so we can enjoy it anytime we want.

This DIY milkshake version of butterbeer is extremely simple to make at home. It turns the butterbeer beverage of the books into a smooth milkshake by using vanilla ice cream and butterscotch. Enjoy!

MAKES 2 SERVINGS

YOU'LL NEED:

- 1^1/$_2$ cups vanilla ice cream
- 3 tablespoons butterscotch syrup
- ^{1}/$_2$ cup cream soda
- Optional: whipped cream
- Optional: 1–2 tablespoons butterscotch chips

DIRECTIONS:

1. Put the vanilla ice cream, butterscotch syrup, and cream soda in a blender. Blend until smooth.
2. Pour the milkshake into two glasses.
3. Top with whipped cream and a sprinkling of butterscotch chips. Serve immediately.

·FUN FOR EVERYONE·

While there is no specific recipe for this called out in the Harry Potter series, it's generally considered to be sweet and frothy with a butterscotch flavor. In the books it's alluded to as being an alcoholic drink. However, at Universal Studios' Wizarding World of Harry Potter in Orlando, Florida, it's served as an icy nonalcoholic drink. Add 1 ounce butterscotch liqueur and omit 2 tablespoons butterscotch syrup for a fun twist!

Make Peanut Butter Cups

What makes for a better combination than chocolate and peanut butter? Reese's Peanut Butter Cups are a forever favorite treat and this taste-alike recipe can be stored in your refrigerator for up to 1 week.

MAKES 8 SERVINGS

YOU'LL NEED:

- 2 tablespoons butter
- 1 tablespoon powdered sugar
- 1 1/2 cups chocolate chips
- 1/2 cup creamy peanut butter, divided
- Pam or oil spray

DIRECTIONS:

1. Fill the bottom of a double boiler with water, and heat until hot but not boiling. (If using a heavy-bottomed pan, skip this step.)
2. Melt the butter in the top of the double broiler (or pan). Once melted, mix in the powdered sugar.
3. Immediately begin adding the chocolate chips. Stir them as they melt to keep the melted chocolate from burning.
4. Once combined, remove from heat.
5. Lightly spray an 8-cup muffin tin with oil to prevent sticking.
6. Place a heaping spoonful of the melted chocolate into each of the muffin cups.
7. Add 1 tablespoon peanut butter on top of each dollop of chocolate.
8. Spoon the remaining chocolate on top of the peanut butter in each cup, distributing it evenly among the muffin cups.
9. Place the tray in the freezer about 2 hours or until solid. Pop the treats out of the muffin tin and enjoy!

Eat Fruit on a Stick

A cute addition to any get-together, fruit skewers are a way to add some color to your party snacks. Not to mention fruits are loaded with fiber, vitamins, minerals, and antioxidants. Plus, whether your guests are vegan, vegetarian, lactose-intolerant, gluten-free, or have a nut allergy, they can all eat fruit! And, fruit skewers are finger food. Really, what's not to like?

MAKES 8 SERVINGS

YOU'LL NEED:

- 2 cups grapes
- 2 cups cubed watermelon
- 1 large apple, cubed
- 1 cup hulled and halved strawberries
- 1 cup blackberries or raspberries

DIRECTIONS:

Slide the fruits onto 8 skewers, alternating them in any order you prefer.

PART 5

FIELD DAY EXTRAVAGANZA

Remember that day every spring in elementary school when classes were canceled in favor of 6 hours of organized recess? Don't you wish you had a day off from work like that? Why not throw it back to those carefree days with your own Field Day Extravaganza! Field days aren't just goofing off or playing hooky. With exciting challenges like mini relays, team events, and skill sports that keep your mind and reflexes sharp, a Field Day Extravaganza is a literal mental—and physical—health day. You have to be ready for anything in today's world!

Kids always seem to have endless energy. (If someone could figure out how to bottle that, I'd buy it in a heartbeat!) Throwing your own Field Day Extravaganza gives you a taste of that stamina because your adrenaline will be pumping all day long. And, you'll be having so much fun you'll completely forget that you're getting in some heart-healthy exercise! Plus, a healthy dose of competition among friends is perfect for strengthening those relationships and making new memories.

You'll have a ball organizing your own field day! Pick out six to ten of the events I've outlined in this section and gather a few small prizes for the winners. You can pack them all in during one day, spread the games over a weekend, or just get together here and there with your friends for field day playdates. However you do it, get your teams together, set a date, and shop for hydrating drinks and healthy snacks—the Field Day Extravaganza is about to begin!

Play Capture the Flag

Can you sneak into enemy territory and return with their precious flag without getting caught? That's the aim of this game, where you put your powers of stealth and agility to the test as you race to outwit the other team and capture the flag!

To play, you'll need a large area, preferably one full of obstructions and obstacles to make the game more challenging. The more places to sneak around, the better! You'll need to have two teams with an even number of players on each side, preferably at least five on each team.

Both teams need their own territory of roughly the same size. Each team will hide its flag deep within their area. No snooping! There also needs to be a designated "jail" area where tagged players of the opposing team will wait for their own team members to rescue them. (Hint: this could be your chance to be the hero.)

Before you set off to hide your flag, here is a rundown of the game rules:

- Once the teams are chosen, each team gets 5 minutes to hide its "flag." (Note: the flag doesn't need to be an actual flag; it can be anything you have on hand, like a scrap of fabric, a small towel, or even a Frisbee.)
- When players of the opposing team are in enemy territory, they can be tagged and sent to jail. There is no limit for how long a player may be in jail, how many times they might be sent to jail, or how many times they can be rescued.
- When players are in jail in the enemy's territory, they can only be rescued by being tagged by a member of their own team.
- If you're tagged carrying the opposing team's flag, you go to jail and the flag is returned to its hiding spot.
- The game ends when one team captures the opposing team's flag and brings it back to their territory.

Hatch an Egg-and-Spoon Race

$$$ | 👤👤👤👤+👤 | 🌳🏠

How's your hand-eye coordination these days? Do you think it's good enough to balance an egg on a spoon while racing against the competition to pass the finish line? It's time to find out if you have what it takes!

Carrying an egg on a spoon doesn't seem all that difficult at first glance. Egg on spoon, spoon in hand, feet dashing across the yard—how hard could it be? Putting your balance to the test is key as you make your way down the course without tripping all over yourself. All it takes is one overzealous step to make that egg go splat!

To play, set up two markers about 50' or so away from each other. One will be the start line and one will be the finish line. Have everyone line up at the start. Give the participants a spoon and an egg to hold out in front of them as they race across the course. On the count of three, the race is on!

If the game's too easy, mix it up. Instead of running, have participants walk backward, hop on one leg, or carry the spoon with their nondominant hand. The first person to cross the finish line with the egg intact and still on the spoon wins.

Play Tug of War

$$$ | 🚶🚶🚶🚶🚶+ | 🌳🏠

Ready, set, pull! The game is on as each team tries its hardest to pull their opponents through the neutral zone and win the contest. With this event, you can really show off all of those hours you've been putting in at the gym! Upper body, core, lower body—you'll need all the strength you've developed to help your team win.

With a long enough rope, you can play Tug of War with as many people as you can find. Tie a scarf around the rope to mark the middle and have the players line up in equal teams on either side. Typically, the strongest person on each team takes the place at the end of the rope, as the anchor. Draw a line in the dirt or use another scarf on the ground as a marker for neutral territory. When the judge says "Pull!" each team tugs as hard as they can until the majority of the opposing team crosses the center line. The game is officially over when the judge declares a winner.

For safety, don't coil the rope around any of your body parts or clothing. Be careful with your grip to prevent rope burn (best to wear gloves). It's all fun and field day until someone gets hurt, and no one wants that. May the strongest team win!

?? POP TRIVIA ??

According to the official rules from the Tug of War International Federation, the game rope should be at least 110' long and 4–5" in diameter, and each team should have eight players. Epic.

Catch 'em All with Red Rover

Gotta catch 'em all! That's not just the theme of Pokémon, it's also the object of Red Rover—the classic field day game where you take advantage of your opponents' weak links. Racing your way across the field, it's full speed ahead as you try your hardest to break through the chain of arms to bring home a new player and celebrate!

Start with two teams of at least six people lined up 20–30' away from each other. Each team links hands to form a line. You're really going to need your grip strength for this one! The teams then take turns saying "Red Rover, Red Rover, send [player's name] over." The chosen player then runs across the distance and attempts to break the linked hands in between any two. (Be mindful of arms and shoulders as too much force from a runner could cause injury.) Pro tip: if you want to win the game, pick the smallest players from the other team to run at you—you can hold them!

If you successfully break the link, you can then pick one of the players you ran into and bring them back over to your team. (Hint: take the stronger one.) You're now one step closer to victory! If you are unsuccessful, however, you then have to join the other team. Where's your loyalty, mate?

The game continues this way until one team has absorbed all the players from the opposing team and they are then declared the winner. Victory is ours!

Toss Water Balloons

Here's a game that calls for quick reflexes and soft hands. The tension mounts as you and your partner toss a water-filled balloon to each other, moving farther apart after each exchange, working toward a wild—but hopefully not wet—finish.

All you need for this competition is balloons, water, and at least two teams of two players. Start with two lines of people facing each other, about 5' apart. Everyone tosses the balloon to their partner at the same time. After each partner has successfully caught the balloon, every person takes one step back and repeats the process. If the balloon breaks, you're out. As the game progresses, you'll slowly move farther and farther apart until there is only one team remaining. The two players left are the water balloon toss champions!

If you want to stay in the game as long as possible, always make sure to catch the balloon with both hands. Gently toss the balloon and don't throw it—you want your partner to be able to catch the balloon in a low, swooping motion. If the balloon comes in too high, the chances of dropping it increase. Kids are usually good at this game because they're low to the ground, but as an adult, your hand-eye coordination has greatly improved, so you'll be able to hang in the game for the longer tosses.

Best to play this game on a hot day, but in any case, make sure to have a change of clothes or a towel nearby—you're probably going to get wet!

FUN FOR EVERYONE

To make it easier for small hands, use eggs instead! The rules for tossing eggs and water balloons remain the same. Except in this version, you may end up with egg on your face.

Giggle Through a Three-Legged Race

Two brains, three legs, what could possibly go wrong? Tying yourself to a friend probably wasn't on the top of your to-do list today, but if you figure out how to stay in sync, winning the race will be a breeze.

The three-legged race is an easy go-to field day activity that's pretty much always on the day's agenda. The simple setup belies the challenging execution, but it's downright hilarious to watch as people hop across the field, often unsuccessfully.

To get ready, one person will tie his right leg to his teammate's left leg with a bandana or scarf. The tie should be tight enough so it won't slip down but loose enough so it doesn't cut off anyone's circulation. Have everyone line up along the start line and set off on the "go" signal. The teams will race (more likely, hobble) down the field to the finish line. The team that crosses the finish line first, wins!

It's hard to learn how to move in sync with someone else, especially because the other person's stride and leg length is probably different from yours. You'll have to work together as a team to accomplish a common goal—aka trying not to fall down. Good luck!

Hop Into the Sack Race

Get in, we're going sack racing! That's probably not something you ever thought you'd say after the age of ten, and especially not to the tune of *Mean Girls*! For this field day event, you and your friends are going feet-first into potato sacks to make your way to the finish line in record time. Big hops or little hops, the person who makes it across the finish line first wins the race. On your mark...get set...hop!

There are a few rules that all participants must abide by for a fair race. First, both feet must be in the sack at all times. If you fall, get back up and have both feet in the sack before you continue. Second, keep the top of your sack up by your waist. If the sack isn't tall enough, the rule is that it must stay above your knees. And finally, one hand has to be holding your potato sack at all times. If at any point you let go, you will be disqualified and can no longer win the race. Don't be that guy!

To make the race last longer, go the relay route or make the racers touch a mark at the far end of the course and then hop back to the beginning. And in the rare event that you don't have potato sacks on hand, any type of burlap sack, pillow case, or trash bag will work fine too. Happy hopping!

Run a Wheelbarrow Race

Arms down, feet up—hang on to your hats, this is going to get tough! The wheelbarrow race involves one person in front walking on her hands and another person behind, holding the first person's feet, wheelbarrow-style. The person on the ground will move across the field using her hands and upper body as the second player guides her along by her feet. Wait. What?

Here's how it works: set up two cones about 20' apart. Have the teams wheelbarrow down to one cone, circle around it, and come back to the start. Whichever team makes it back first, wins. For an easier variation, have the players switch positions when they get to the cone. Doing this will make it a little less strenuous on each player's wrists and shoulders. If you have a lot of teams, you can work this one by bracket, sending two teams at a time, with the winners of each round pairing off against each other until you have one winner.

Benefits of this game include improving your upper-body strength, coordination, communication, and teamwork skills.

Add to Your Bucket List: The Car Wash Relay

Can you fill a bucket fast? How about doing it only using a sponge? I thought so! In this game, you race back and forth down the field as you compete to see who can fill up their bucket the fastest using water carried in a sponge.

To play, start by breaking into even teams. Place several buckets of water near the start line where all teams can access them easily, as well as a large sponge for each team. Place one empty bucket about 20' away for each team.

On the signal, the first person of the relay from each team dunks the sponge into a bucket of water, soaking it. Next, they'll run down the field, where they'll squeeze as much water as possible out of the sponge into their team's bucket. Then, they run back to the start line where they'll pass off the sponge to the next players, who repeat the process. After 3 minutes, the team that has the fullest bucket wins the relay!

Do Some Hula-Hoopin'

Spinning a Hula-Hoop around your waist may look easy, but it's quite the challenge to move your hips just so to keep up the sustained momentum. Have you got the rhythm? Compete with each other to see who can keep the hoop up the longest in an elimination-style challenge. Players will face off one on one. The first player to drop her hoop loses! Shake that money-maker (or something like that).

For a big group, make it a team challenge with the Hula Circle game variation. Have everyone form a large circle and hold hands. Have two players link hands through a Hula-Hoop. The goal is to move the Hula-Hoop around the circle without unlinking hands or letting the Hula-Hoop touch the ground. Make it more competitive by using two hoops. Put them directly across from each other and see if your group can move them around the circle without the hoops catching up to each other.

You could also split into two even groups and race to see who can get the hoop around the circle fastest without letting go of each other's hands. Get your hoop on!

·FUN FOR EVERYONE·

If Hula-Hoops aren't quite your style, opt for a riveting game of Cornhole (aka bean bag toss) instead! This game is a favorite at tailgates and will be a perfect addition to your Field Day Extravaganza.

Play Mega Ring Toss

Have those Hula-Hoops play double duty for a life-sized game of ring toss! Put your aim to the test as you try to land the hoops in the right spot to earn as many points as possible.

For this challenge you'll need six cones and four Hula-Hoops. Set up the cones in a 3-2-1 formation about a foot apart. Have the players stand 10–20' away and toss the Hula-Hoops toward the cones.

For scoring, you get one point for every Hula-Hoop that lands on a cone in the row of three; two points for every hoop that lands on a cone in the row of two; and three points for every hoop that lands on the cone in the row of one. Have a notepad handy to keep score. After everyone's taken their turn, the player with the most points wins. If there's a tie, have the players each throw another round of hoops from an additional 5' away to break the tie and determine a champion. If the game is too easy, increase the distance you'll have to throw or play with a smaller hoop or ring.

Play Human Hungry, Hungry Hippos

Chomp, chomp, chomp—how hungry is your hippo? Do your best to snag up as many balls as you can in one bite! You can bring this board game to life easily with just a few materials.

The goal of the game is to be the hippo who collects the most balls in the shortest amount of time. In this game designed for eight players, you'll need to rely on teamwork to collect the most balls in 30 seconds.

To play you'll need the following:

- A large room or open space with a smooth floor
- 100 ball pit balls
- 4 skateboards
- 4 buckets

1. Start by marking the center of your game space. You'll also want to mark four corners equidistant from the center to prevent cheating.
2. Dump all the balls in the middle of your large, open space.
3. Have players split into four teams of two and go to a corner behind the markings.
4. One player lays facedown on a skateboard holding a bucket while the other player stands behind him holding onto his ankles. This is how you will slide across the floor like a hippo!
5. On the count of three, you have 30 seconds to slide into the middle, collect as many balls as possible using only your bucket, and slide back to your position. Repeat as many times as possible within 30 seconds. Good luck!

Get Dizzy, Lizzy

$$$ | ♟♟♟♟+♟ | 🌳🏠

How quickly can you run after you've spun around ten times? That's what you're taking on in the Dizzy Lizzy relay race. Walking in a straight line has never been more challenging (except maybe after a few glasses of wine).

Start by splitting into two even teams and setting up your game by placing two lines (a start line and an activity line) about 20' apart from each other. You'll need two broomsticks or whiffle ball bats to place on the activity line.

Players run down to the broomstick or whiffle ball bat, hold it upright in their hands with one end on the ground, and then place their forehead on the top end so that they are looking down at the ground. They then spin around ten times, drop the broomstick or bat, and run back to their team to tag the next player. Be careful, you're going to be a Dizzy Lizzy on the way back. Be the first team to have everyone make it back and you win. Good luck—the room might be spinning for a while!

Stomp a Balloon

This game is not only fun, but it's a great way to get out some aggression. Just be sure to only stomp the balloons! Here's how it works: do your best to pop other players' balloons while protecting your own. Last one standing with an intact balloon takes home the gold. The catch is each player's balloon is attached to one of his feet by a piece of string—and you can't hold it. You have to run around and dodge other players while trying to take them out the game

You'll need minimal materials for this one—only string and enough balloons for all players. Blow up the appropriate number of balloons and tie one to each player's foot with a piece of string. I also recommend playing indoors; it's much easier to sweep or vacuum up the popped balloon pieces instead of picking them up out of grass. And the more players you have, the better. It's great for all ages, from young children to grandparents.

Hop Along on the Great Kangaroo Race

What hops, has a pouch, and lives in the Land Down Under? The kangaroo, of course! Put your own hopping skills to the test and see if you have what it takes to win the Great Kangaroo Race.

Each player will need a tennis ball, whiffle ball, or baseball. The smaller the object, the harder the race will be. Have all players line up at the start line and place the ball between their knees. On three, the players have to hop their way down the line, around a cone, and back to the start line without dropping the ball. If you drop the ball, you have to go all the way back to the start line and begin again.

Make it more challenging and use a balloon. If the balloon pops, it's game over for you. Hip to the hop and don't let your ball drop!

Untie Yourself

Contort yourself underneath arms and around elbows, twisting backward and forward to undo the tangle that you and your teammates have created. You'll have to work together before time runs out to straighten out the circle and call it a victory!

To play, have everyone stand next to each other forming a large circle. Then, each player holds hands with another player with one major catch—you cannot hold the hand of the person next to you. Reach across the circle to grab the hands of other players. And hold on tight. If you let go even one time, you've failed the challenge. Once everyone is holding hands, the group has been turned into a giant human knot! Now, the challenge is to un-knot yourselves without releasing hands. Success depends on patience, group strategy, and a fair amount of body contortions.

The bigger the group, the better. It's family-friendly and makes a great game for reunions. Have two groups compete against each other to see who can untangle their group the quickest.

Run the Don't Spill the Beans! Relay

You don't have to keep any secrets in this race, you only have to make sure you don't spill the beans before you make it to the finish line. In this team relay, you'll be carrying a spoonful of dried beans across a field—but you won't be walking or running—you have to hop on one foot.

Use your balance and speed to outpace your opponents! Dip into the bowl of beans with your spoon and holding it upright and as steady as possible, begin hopping on one foot toward your team's bowl at the other end of the field. Dump your beans in the bowl and rush back to pass off the spoon to the next player. The race isn't over until every team finishes. The team with the most beans in their bowl is the winner.

Keep a Level Head

This challenge is the ultimate test in balance. Keep your head as steady as possible to avoid spilling a cup of water all over yourself!

Have the players lie down on the floor, face up. Give them each a paper cup half-filled with water. When the game starts, have them place the cup on their forehead and let go. The goal is to sit up without spilling the water or losing the cup. You have to keep your head back and perfectly balanced to keep from turning into a soggy mess.

Shake Your Sillies Out

This one is just plain silly fun—but still competitive. Take two large, empty tissue boxes or similar-sized boxes with an opening on the front (top). On the back of each, cut two slits approximately 4–5" inches apart. Slide a belt through each of the boxes and fill them with Ping-Pong balls. A player from each team straps the belt around their waist and at the signal, shakes and wiggles until the balls all fall out of the box. The first one to empty their box wins.

Play Kick the Can

Can you guard the treasure from all directions? Let's find out! A cool combination of tag and capture the flag, Kick the Can is all about protecting what's yours. When you're not "it," it's your job to "kick the can" and rescue a player that was sent to jail. It's up to you to save the day!

Start by choosing an "it" player. Stand a tin can upright—this is what the "it" player must protect at all costs. When the game begins, everyone who's not "it" must try to kick the can over. If you get tagged by the "it" player you're sent to jail and can't play until someone rescues you. To rescue a player from the game, all you have to do is kick the can over. The game ends when all players have been sent to jail and the can remains standing tall. This game is fast-paced but it can take a while to determine a winner.

Have Four Times the Fun: The Medley

This event isn't like your typical race—it's four races rolled into one! Take on your friends in the ultimate challenge of balance and endurance as you compete for bragging rights. I hope you packed your running shoes!

Set up two cones per player about 30' away from each other. For each event, you must loop around the cone completely before you begin the next event. On "go," you'll crab walk down the field. To crab walk, put your hands on the ground behind you and face up toward the sky, moving on all fours toward your destination. Don't rush yourself or you'll fall over! When you loop around the cone, stand up and hop backward on one foot. When you loop around the cone again, face forward and skip down to the cone on the other side of the field. And finally, for the last leg of the medley, sprint as fast as you can back to the finish line. Zoom, zoom, zoom—the race is on!

Play Flashlight Tag

$ $ $ | 👤👤👤👤👤+ | 🌳 🏠

Dashing through the dark as you run and hide from "It"? It's not a Stephen King novel—it's Flashlight Tag! (Whew.) Running around at night without drawing attention to yourself is the perfect way to end your field day. The dusky evening shadows add a certain edge to this game—it's fun, but also has shades of *Blair Witch Project*. Between the scary and the running and the laughing your head off when you're discovered—or doing the revealing—Flashlight Tag is great exercise and the best stress reliever!

Now, there are two basic ways to play Flashlight Tag under the cover of darkness. First, you could combine it with the typical game of tag where the person identified by flashlight becomes "it" and the flashlight is handed off. Make sure you call "No tag backs!" before handing the flashlight off. Another alternative is to play so that the person who is "it" has to catch all of her players in the beam of her light. Once a player has been tagged, she'll go and wait in a designated area until all the players have been caught (or the "it" player gives up) and you can start a new game. Last person to be found (or not found), wins, and then everybody heads to the fire pit for s'mores.

Take it to the next level and keep the game fair by making the rules tougher. When the "it" player tags the hiding player with the light, he has to identify the player by name for the tag to count. Tag, you're it!

PART 6
A CAMPING WE WILL GO

Summer's here and that means the time has come for you to pack your trunk and head to summer camp! Sleep-away camp was a rite of passage for many growing up. It might have been scary to be away for the first time, but any homesickness quickly vanished when you realized how much fun you would be having 24-7. Campers spent their days playing games, acing challenge courses, doing arts and crafts, creating music, performing in shows, and best of all, bunking with their best friends.

Bringing this special time back to life means you get all the best parts of camp (games, stargazing, swimming) without the lousy ones (buh-bye crazy-big spiders and cold showers). Adult summer camp experiences of all kinds now await you, from spa-like yoga camps to more traditional types—but with gourmet food, air-conditioned cabins, and no counselors cramping your style.

You can bring the camp experience back to life by attending one of these ready-made camps for adults or creating your own immersive camp weekend away with your friends. But, really, you can bring back those good old summer camp memories anytime by organizing the activities and games or making the recipes in this section. Recipes are listed first, because camp makes me hungry. Now let's get started—I call top bunk!

Bake Gourmet S'mores

When you think of camp, what comes to mind first? For most people, it's s'mores. Who can forget crunching on a graham cracker filled with rich, melty chocolate mixed with a sweet gooey marshmallow you roasted yourself over an open fire until it was golden brown (or in flames)?

Even if going to camp only reminds you of mosquitos and uncomfortable sleeping positions, this recipe is guaranteed to change that. These easy-to-make gourmet s'mores don't even require a fire! All you need is your oven and 5 minutes to enjoy this tasty treat.

MAKES 8 SERVINGS

YOU'LL NEED:

- 16 graham cracker halves (8 graham crackers)
- 2 regular-sized bars Hershey's Milk Chocolate or gourmet chocolate bars with raspberry or caramel filling
- 8 regular-sized marshmallows

DIRECTIONS:

1. Preheat the oven to 400°F.
2. Place 8 graham cracker halves in a 9" × 9" pan or on a baking sheet.
3. Place 2–3 pieces of the chocolate (depending on the size of the chocolate squares) on each graham cracker.
4. Place a marshmallow on each chocolate-covered graham cracker.
5. Bake 3–5 minutes, keeping an eye on the marshmallows. Remove from the oven when the marshmallows begin to brown and the chocolate is melting.
6. Place the remaining graham crackers on top of each s'more.
7. Allow to cool 1–2 minutes before eating, as the chocolate and marshmallow will be hot.

DIY Some Trail Mix

Trail mix is one of those easy, filling snacks that is perfect to take with you on the go. The nuts and seeds give you energy to win all your camp competitions while dried fruit or chocolate satisfies your sweet tooth. Yum!

There is no "perfect" trail mix recipe. It's really all up to how sweet or savory each camper wants her trail mix to be.

MAKES 12 SERVINGS

YOU'LL NEED:

- 2 cups nuts (almonds, walnuts, peanuts, cashews, pistachios, hazelnuts, and/or pecans)
- 1 cup seeds (sunflower, pumpkin, flax, hemp, pine nuts, and/or chia are great options)
- 2 cups dried fruit (mangos, raisins, cherries, peaches, figs, dates, apples, cranberries, and/or pears)
- 1 cup mix-ins (white chocolate, milk chocolate, dark chocolate, cocoa nibs, mini marshmallows, your favorite candy, pretzels, cereal, granola, wasabi peas, coconut flakes, espresso beans, etc.)
- Optional: spices of your choice to taste (sea salt, cinnamon, chili powder, ginger, cardamom, cayenne pepper, nutmeg, etc.)

DIRECTIONS:

1. Place all the ingredients in separate bowls.
2. Assign a tablespoon (measuring spoon or similar-sized table spoon) so campers can measure out their own custom blend of trail mix.
3. They'll want to combine 2–3 tablespoons nuts, 2–3 tablespoons seeds, 1–3 tablespoons mix-ins, and a pinch of spice to round out the flavors. To make $1/2$ cup trail mix per serving, campers should aim for filling up their bags with about 8 tablespoons total from all ingredients.

Stuff Pigs in a Blanket

These simple treats will take you back to a much simpler time—when all you had to worry about was going to bed after dinner and not doing the dishes!

MAKES 8 SERVINGS

YOU'LL NEED:

- 8 Pillsbury Crescents
- 8 slices cheese (I suggest sharp Cheddar for a twist, but American cheese is standard)
- 8 hot dogs

DIRECTIONS:

1. Preheat oven to 375°F. Line a baking sheet with aluminum foil.
2. Lay out the crescent rolls on the prepared baking sheet. Place a piece of cheese and a hot dog on top of each.
3. Roll up each crescent roll, wrapping the dough around the cheese and hot dog. Space out the rolls evenly on the baking sheet.
4. Bake 12–15 minutes until cooked through.

Fire Up Some Nachos

$$$ | ♀♀♀♀♀+ | 🌳🏠

It's not your average Tuesday; it's Nacho Tuesday! Could this get any cheesier? (The answer is yes, it can.) If you're a vegetarian, just skip the meat in this recipe.

Campfire Nachos are the perfect camp food. They're easy to make over a fire on a camping stove or on your stove at home. They can be eaten with your hands and require only one pan to cook them in. It's not a bad night to have dish duty!

Whether you're craving nachos for a snack or a meal, this recipe is easily doubled or tripled to feed a crowd. Plus, you can also get totally creative with the toppings—they're your nachos!

MAKES 4 SERVINGS

YOU'LL NEED:

- 1 pound ground beef, shredded chicken, or shredded pork
- 1½ tablespoons olive oil
- ½ pound tortilla chips
- 1–2 cups Mexican cheese blend (or cheese of your choice—sharp Cheddar, Colby, Monterey Jack, and Pepper Jack all work well)

Optional:

- 1 (15-ounce) can black beans
- 1 (15-ounce) can refried beans
- 1 medium jalapeño pepper, sliced
- 1 medium avocado, sliced
- 1 cup guacamole or mashed avocado
- 1 medium red onion, sliced
- 1 handful chopped cilantro
- 1 cup salsa or pico de gallo
- 1 medium tomato, diced
- Spices of your choice (cumin, chili powder, salt, cayenne pepper)
- Hot sauce

DIRECTIONS:

1. Start by cooking the meat in your preferred manner. The meat needs to be fully cooked before making your nachos.
2. Heat the oil in a large cast-iron pan or Dutch oven with a lid.
3. If using a stove, heat the pan over medium heat. If using a fire, place the pan on a metal grill and carefully monitor the chips while cooking to make sure they don't burn. If they start to burn, move the pan away from the direct fire.
4. When the pan is hot, spread about $1/3$–$1/2$ of the chips along the bottom of the pan.
5. Cover with about $1/3$ of the cheese and the optional toppings of your choice. Use a wooden spoon to spread the cheese and toppings over the chips so that everything cooks evenly.
6. Cover that with a light layer of chips, about $1/4$–$1/3$ of the remaining chips.
7. Sprinkle about $1/3$ of the shredded cheese on top of the chips. Spread another set of your chosen toppings across the cheese.
8. Add the remaining chips, cheese, and toppings.
9. Cover with the lid and cook over medium heat about 10–12 minutes until the cheese has melted and the chips are crisp. Scoop servings onto individual plates and dive in.

Eat Sloppy Joes

You'll want to keep napkins and Wet Ones on hand for this recipe! Sloppy joes are a camp cook's go-to because they're so easy to make en masse. Perfect for when you have a large crowd to feed!

When I think of sloppy joes, the first thing that comes to mind is Ashley Olsen as Alyssa in the 1995 film *It Takes Two*. She plays a rich girl who happens to look exactly like an orphan named Amanda. The two switch places—Amanda ends up at Alyssa's piano recital and Alyssa ends up at an overnight camp where she isn't sure how to eat a sloppy joe because she's never had one.

She begins by eating daintily and her new friends watch, not sure how to react. Kirstie Alley's character, Diane, asks Alyssa what's wrong with her, exclaiming that sloppy joes are her favorite. Upon hearing that, she digs in, making a mess of herself, and the room erupts in applause. Sloppy joes are just that good. Here's how to make your own.

MAKES 4 SERVINGS

YOU'LL NEED:

- 1 pound lean ground beef
- $^{1}/_{2}$ medium white onion, peeled and diced
- 1 medium green bell pepper, seeded and diced
- 2 teaspoons minced garlic
- 1 teaspoon kosher salt, or to taste
- $^{1}/_{4}$ teaspoon black pepper
- $^{3}/_{4}$ cup water, divided (or more as needed)
- $^{1}/_{2}$ cup ketchup

- 1–2 teaspoons apple cider vinegar
- 1–2 teaspoons Dijon mustard
- $1/4$ teaspoon Worcestershire sauce
- 1 tablespoon brown sugar
- 4 hamburger buns

DIRECTIONS:

1. Begin by placing the ground beef and onion in a 10" skillet over medium heat. Cook, stirring until the beef is cooked all the way through and the onions are translucent.
2. Add the green pepper, garlic, salt, and black pepper and stir 4–5 minutes.
3. Pour in about $1/4$ cup water to prevent sticking and to help the peppers soften.
4. Add the ketchup, vinegar, mustard, Worcestershire sauce, and brown sugar; stir to combine.
5. Add the remaining $1/2$ cup water and stir. Reduce the heat to low and allow the mixture to simmer 30–45 minutes or until it has thickened. Add more water if necessary to achieve the sloppy joe consistency.
6. Remove from heat and serve on hamburger buns.

Dig Into Skillet Brownies

$ $ $ | 👤👤👤👤👤+ | 🌳🏠

While s'mores are a favorite camping delight, there are other decadent treat options that will make your taste buds sing camp songs with joy! This Skillet Brownie recipe is so incredibly easy to make and a great alternative for when you don't have an oven handy. Enjoy your Skillet Brownie with a cold glass of milk or a scoop of vanilla ice cream for an extra treat. Tasty!

MAKES 10 SERVINGS

YOU'LL NEED:

- $1/2$ (18.4-ounce) box Pillsbury Chocolate Fudge Brownie Mix
- 1 large egg
- $1/3$ cup vegetable or canola oil
- $1/8$ cup water

DIRECTIONS:

1. Add all the ingredients to a large cast-iron pan and mix thoroughly, making sure to spread out the mixture evenly.
2. Place the pan over the campfire (or on a stove burner over medium heat) and cook 20–25 minutes.
3. Brownies are ready when the edges turn crisp and begin to pull away from the pan and the middle of the mixture is no longer runny.
4. Remove from heat and let cool 5–10 minutes.

★ PRO TIP ★

This Skillet Brownie recipe can be made with any kind of brownie mix. Simply halve the recipe measurements on the box and follow the same cooking method listed here. Add your favorite toppings (such as M&M's, Reese's Peanut Butter Cup Minis, or gummy bears) for a one-of-a-kind dessert!

Grill Out

Whether you're at sleepaway camp or simply pitching a tent in your backyard, throwing some protein on the grill is a must to complete the day. Grilling makes less mess than frying in the kitchen, plus it's easier to cook up a meal for a group of people.

Luckily you can grill almost anything to suit everyone's tastes and dietary restrictions. Gluten-free buns to the rescue! Set up a bar for your grill-out and include chicken, hot dogs, cheeseburgers, and veggie skewers or burgers. Put out some condiments, plus lettuce, tomato, onions, cheese, and avocado slices. Complete the set-up with chips and you're good to go. Throw some fresh peaches on the grill to make a sweet treat for the health-conscious. For those who want to indulge, make a big skillet brownie or whip out those long skewers for roasting marshmallows and keep the chocolate and graham crackers handy. You've now got the perfect camp meal—bon appétit!

Cook Oatmeal over an Open Fire

Forget packets. Forget "quick cooking." This way of making oatmeal will get you fired up! Oatmeal has been the go-to energy-packed breakfast food for generations. It's loaded with protein and slow-digesting carbs that will keep you full on your hikes and nature scavenger hunt adventures.

MAKES 1 SERVING

YOU'LL NEED:

- 1 cup water
- $\frac{1}{2}$ cup rolled oats (not instant or quick)
- 2 tablespoons honey
- 1 teaspoon ground cinnamon
- Optional: raisins, fruit, or shredded coconut

DIRECTIONS:

1. Pour the water into a medium saucepan or cast-iron skillet and bring to a boil.
2. Add the oats and reduce heat (if using a campfire, move the pan higher away from the flames). Stir to prevent sticking.
3. Once the water is absorbed, remove from heat.
4. Stir in the honey and cinnamon.
5. Add the toppings of your choice if desired. Spoons up!

Catch Tuna on Crackers

Next to peanut butter and jelly, tuna is one of the easiest protein-packed snacks to keep with you. It makes for a wholesome and filling lunch or a great tide-you-over snack on the go. Plus its simplicity is reminiscent of childhood. Unless you hated tuna. In that case, you can also make this recipe with canned or shredded chicken. Mix up the spices to change the flavor, top it with half a cherry tomato or an avocado slice, and you have yourself a fancy little treat!

MAKES 10 SERVINGS

YOU'LL NEED:

- 1 (6-ounce) can tuna
- ¼ cup mayonnaise or plain Greek yogurt
- Spices to taste (salt, pepper, parsley, dried onion)
- 20 round crackers of your choice

DIRECTIONS:

1. Mix the tuna, mayonnaise or Greek yogurt, and spices together in a bowl using a fork.
2. Spread the tuna across the crackers. Enjoy!

Bake Homemade Granola

This isn't like your average store-bought granola. It's even better, because it includes all the good stuff, none of the bad stuff (we're looking at you, excess refined sugar and preservatives), and is perfectly customizable.

MAKES 8 SERVINGS (ABOUT 2 CUPS TOTAL)

YOU'LL NEED:

- 2 cups instant oats
- 1 cup dried fruit of your choice
- $1/2$ cup seeds of your choice
- 1 cup nuts of your choice
- $1/2$ cup maple syrup or honey
- 2–3 tablespoons coconut oil
- 2 tablespoons brown sugar
- Optional: 2–3 teaspoons spices of your choice

> ★ PRO TIP ★
>
> Granola can be made sweet or savory simply depending on your choice of ingredients. Brown rice or quinoa flavored with kale chips, olives, curry or saffron, chili flakes or jalapeños, plus nuts and poppy or sesame seeds gives you just as much nutrition and energy without the sweetness.

DIRECTIONS:

1. Preheat the oven to 300°F.
2. In a bowl, combine the oats, dried fruit, seeds, and nuts.
3. In a separate bowl, mix together the maple syrup or honey, coconut oil, brown sugar, and optional spices.
4. Pour the liquid into the dry oat mixture making sure to evenly coat all the ingredients.
5. Lay parchment paper on a baking sheet. Spread the granola mixture evenly across the pan.
6. Bake 40 minutes, tossing the granola about halfway through to ensure even cooking.
7. Allow the granola to cool 5–10 minutes. Store in an airtight container.

Design a Galaxy in a Jar

This project combines two favorite camp activities: stargazing and rainy day arts and crafts. Bring the stars indoors when you make these multi-dimensional galaxy jars! (Awesome '70s/'80s mix tape optional.)

YOU'LL NEED:

- 1 (100-count) pack of cotton balls
- 1 (16-ounce) Mason jar with 1-piece lid
- Paint in 2–3 colors (acrylic or tempera work well)
- Silver or holographic glitter (any color will work, though)
- Water, as needed

DIRECTIONS:

1. Pull the cotton balls apart. Next, start packing them, firmly but not too tightly, into the bottom of the jar until the layer is about 1–1¹/₂" thick. This is layer one.
2. Put 3–5 drops of paint over the cotton. Add a sprinkle of glitter, lightly covering the cotton.
3. Add just enough water to cover the layer of cotton, paint, and glitter. Put the lid on the jar and shake until combined. Take off the lid and use a straw or spoon to push down the cotton again, creating an even layer.
4. Repeat these steps for the remaining layers until the jar is full.
5. When finished, screw the lid on tightly and enjoy your galaxy!

Make Pom-Pom Pen Holders

Remember when you had to write letters—yes, letters!—home to your family from camp? For some of us, this was before email existed (or was available at camp), not to mention smartphones. Even though you no longer send messages to your parents about frogs in your bed or the yucky camp food—at least, not with pen and paper—spend a morning getting crafty and using your imagination to create a trendy but practical piece of decor for your "writing" desk. Pom-poms are having a trendy moment and thank goodness. From fashion to home decor, they're everywhere. It's just like the '70s all over again! These cute little fluff balls were adorable on the back of your socks and they'll be downright fabulous on your desk as well.

YOU'LL NEED:

- Hot glue gun
- Pom-poms in all colors and sizes
- A rinsed-out tin can or a glass Mason jar

DIRECTIONS:

To make your pen holder simply use your hot glue gun to glue the pom-poms all over the tin can or glass jar. It's a great way to up-cycle some food containers as well! Allow yourself to play around with patterns, color, and size to create unique designs.

Paint Pet Rocks

What doesn't move, requires no responsibility on your part, and is the perfect gift for someone allergic to animals? A Pet Rock, duh.

The Pet Rock first emerged in 1975 and was marketed, of course, as the perfect pet. There's no need to clean up after them, no need to feed them or take them on a walk. Naturally, your Pet Rock will give you minimal companionship, though, so it's really up to you if it's worth the investment or not.

Even though Pet Rocks can be bought, they can also be DIYed! All you'll need to create these stony sidekicks are rocks (preferably smooth), acrylic paint, and small paintbrushes. Also consider googly eyes, tufts of fake fur (for hair), and mini pom-poms or other craft supplies, plus craft glue.

To make this a real campy project, start by hunting for rocks in your yard, by the water, or at a nearby park (make sure it's okay to take rocks from public spaces). Choose a rock based on what you want your pet to look like, or let the rock serve as inspiration. Maybe you'd like a whole litter of rocks, or a rock band? Once you've brought your pets-to-be home, grab your paint colors and get to it! You can start by painting the rock with one color or just start with features. Create a rock that looks like you. Paint it a crazy color or make it realistic, like the puppy you wish you had. Let your imagination run wild!

Once you've completed your Pet Rock, why not make another (or several) and spread a little inspiration around the world by participating in the Kindness Rocks Project? Visit TheKindnessRocksProject.com for more information.

POP TRIVIA

Pet Rocks came back on the market in 2012 and are available to purchase for a cool $19.95.

Slip 'N Slide Away

Slipping and sliding your way down a water-slicked hill is the best way to cool off on a hot afternoon, and it's not just for kids. Make a mad dash as you get a running head start and hurl yourself down the slippery slide. Go down backward for an extra challenge. Bombs away!

DIY your own grown-up Slip 'N Slide using just a few materials.

YOU'LL NEED:

- A long tarp or plastic sheet (about 10' × 100')
- Environmentally safe dish soap
- A hose connected to a water source

DIRECTIONS:

Stretch your tarp or plastic sheeting out across a flat area. Put your water slide on a hill if you want to build up some extra speed. Make sure there are no rocks or sharp objects underneath or at the bottom of the slide. Spread some dish soap from one end to the other. This acts as a lubricant to keep you moving. Connect the hose to the water source, place it at the top of the slide, and turn it on. Once the water is running down to the bottom, you're good to go!

Make Moves Like Katniss

$$$ | 👫 + 👪 | 🌳 🏠

Can you nail the bull's-eye? Find out when you put your aim to the test on the archery range. This ultimate camp sport (and Hunger Games skill) is a test of upper-body strength, aim, and eyesight. May the odds be ever in your favor!

Whether you fancy yourself Katniss, Legolas, or even Robin Hood, role-playing is fun and archery builds strength. Get your group together and head to a local archery range for a lesson from an instructor. You'll test your discipline and focus as you pull back and release at just the right moment to send the arrow soaring into the target. If you have the space to safely set up a range at home, why not purchase your own bow and arrow for fun? Ready, aim, fire!

Tell Campfire Stories

Think you're too old for ghost stories? Think again! When it's pitch dark out with only the flickering campfire to light your faces, tales of haunted houses, zombies in a graveyard, or rogue witches can still send chills up your spine. You might have to hang onto the person next to you for dear life! Raise the goose bump factor by hosting your tell-a-thon in a remote area in the woods, desert, or beach—not in your backyard.

Spooky campfire tales aren't just good for giving you the heebie-jeebies or an excuse to snuggle up to the person next to you (choose your seat wisely, my friend). Hearing a creepy story—rather than watching it—makes it more frightening because your imagination fills in the details. And revving up the old imagination boosts creativity. Plus, going through a scary experience with a group of people bonds you. Believe it or not, screaming together in the darkness over a common fear creates a shared experience that ultimately makes us feel less alone in the world. Though, if you need to sleep with your teddy bear tonight, it's okay. I won't tell.

Tie-Dye T-Shirts

Red, yellow, blue—which colors will you choose? Tie-dyeing is an awesome craft that brings out the creative kid in us all. There's a certain finesse to creating stunning patterns and turning a blank canvas into a uniquely colorful garment. But honestly, even if you don't create a perfect spiral, you'll still be proud to wear your me-made shirt.

Pick up a tie-dye kit from a local craft store, get some plain white T-shirts, and let your creative flag fly! There's no limit to the way you mix and match colors. Plus, this activity is great for all ages. Bring enough shirts and dye for everyone at your next family reunion or summer get-together. That way everyone can take home their own colorful and unique souvenir to remember the day by.

Pitch a Tent

At sleepaway camp, you might have stayed in bunks, but on the occasional night that you found yourself out in the wilderness, a tent was what protected you from the elements. Getting out of the house and into the fresh air will brighten your mood and get you back to basics!

Invite your friends over for a sleepover under the stars complete with a tent, sleeping bags, and flashlights. Try to make it an electronics-free outing, like the old days. Pass the time by telling stories (about ghosts, college days, or bad dates), point out constellations, play Flashlight Tag, and eat snacks. Make friendship bracelets to remind you of the night spent out under nature's ceiling. If you make it through the night, reward yourselves by going out to breakfast!

Take a Hike

Stepping outdoors and getting your sweat on is the perfect way to spend a morning before the sun heats up. Round up your fellow campers, grab your hiking boots, and set out on the trail after a hearty breakfast of open-fire oatmeal. Make it a survival of the fittest by awarding a prize to the person (or team) who gets to the top of the trail first. Or, make it a scavenger challenge, with a list of items each person or team has to find and photograph before the hike is over, like a butterfly, a heart-shaped rock, white mushroom, and so on. The sense of accomplishment from summiting that mountain before you take on an afternoon of adventures and crafting will keep your spirits up and give you confidence!

.FUN FOR EVERYONE.

Instead of taking a hike, go to a nearby nature center where there are short trails and signs pointing out facts about the local wildlife and landscapes.

Head to the Swimming Hole

Taking a dip in the cool water of a local swimming hole is the best way to cool off after a long hike! It's also a great way to blow off steam with your buddies when you take a mental health day from work. This is no lap swim at the Y. A swimming hole is where you race to be the first to cannonball into the water and make a splash. After all, the fastest way to get adjusted to cold water is to go all in. No old-fashioned swimming hole nearby? Head to a public pool or find a pool-owning friend.

Challenge your friends to see who can hold their breath the longest, do an underwater handstand, or do the best backflip into the drink! Bring pool noodles or floats and spend the afternoon lazing around. Pack a towel, a good book or chess board, and some snacks for when you take a break to enjoy the sun.

Ride Horseback

Trotting around the ring—or down the trail—as you make friends with your horse is a typical summer camp activity. Once you got the hang of it, you could imagine yourself a cowpoke, a circus performer, one of the Elves of Rivendell, or a character in *Princess Gwenevere and the Jewel Riders*—or any other horse-related fantasy figure of your dreams. Sadly, camp's often the last time we get that close to a horse.

But it needn't be. You can get back in the saddle, riding along with the wind in your hair, on a trail ride or riding lesson geared to adults. Even if you're a city dweller, there's usually a riding facility within a short train or car ride.

A nice cool evening or weekend afternoon spent riding a horse through the countryside will relax you and take your mind off all the stress you've been under. Trail and school horses are selected for gentleness, but you'll still have to pay attention to how you sit and steer—and the horse's reaction. This will make you focus— a form of meditation. This time spent bonding with a powerful animal will keep you attentive and give you confidence. It may even spur you on to more riding lessons. After your ride, make sure to reward your horse with a good brushing and some fresh water and hay, and be sure to clean and put away the tack for the next rider. If nothing else, you'll get some fun shots for *Instagram*.

Bond with Friendship Bracelets

Are you really friends if you haven't made a friendship bracelet together? Of course you are! But there is something really special about wearing a sign of friendship in a pattern you designed together. Wouldn't it be heartwarming to look down at your wrist when you're having a bad day and see a handmade reminder of your loyal bestie?

To make a braided friendship bracelet, you'll need three strands of brightly colored string, such as embroidery floss, about 6–9" long (depending on your wrist size). Line up the three pieces of string. Tie one end of the strings in a knot, about $\frac{1}{2}$" from the end. Begin braiding from the knot toward the other end of the strings.

Once you're at the end, lay your wrist across the string. Have your friend knot the two ends of the bracelet around your wrist where it will stay until it falls off or you cut it off. Friends—and friendship bracelets—forever!

Send Snail Mail

If you thought writing letters by hand was a thing of the past, think again! (And no, my grandmother didn't make me say that.) Nothing says you care like writing a letter to a sweet friend or relative just to let her know you're thinking of her.

Get a group of friends together and gather some art supplies (construction paper or card stock, scissors, glue, colorful pens, and cutouts) to make a ton of cards to send throughout the year. And make sure to bring snacks—crafting is hard work.

Together you can design a plethora of holiday and birthday cards to send to each other or other friends and family. In the days before technology, we had to sit down and handwrite one another letters. It takes time and effort to really do that! A handwritten note in a handmade card is something to be treasured. Don't forget the stamps—there are lots of fun ones to choose from!

DIY Pinecone Bird Feeders

Nature crafts are an essential part of the camp experience. And this craft will keep nature in your life long past the day you make it. It's easy to create these cute DIY bird feeders to hang in your yard or on your balcony. With them, you'll keep your yard hopping with wildlife activity. Pinecone bird feeders are especially fun to make with your own kids or nieces and nephews as you teach them about the nature of your local area. Plus, you get to feel like a kid again, making something helpful and getting closer to nature.

YOU'LL NEED:

- String
- 3 medium pinecones
- 6 tablespoons creamy peanut butter
- 2–3 cups birdseed

DIRECTIONS:

1. Start by wrapping string around the top of each pinecone to create a loop. This will allow you to hang the bird feeders from tree branches.
2. Spread about 2 tablespoons peanut butter all over each pinecone.
3. Pour the birdseed onto a plate. Roll the pinecones in the birdseed, coating them as evenly as possibly. Lightly shake the pinecones over the plate to remove any excess birdseed. Note: resist the urge to make these feeders *Instagram*-worthy. The birds won't care!
4. Find a lovely spot to hang the bird feeders outside and watch as the birds flock to them!

   Happy bird-watching!

Frame Yourself in Nature

Take all your snapshots and memories home from your time at camp and keep them in a nature picture frame! It's the perfect way to display your photos of everyone around the campfire eating nachos, making s'mores, or careening down your epic water slide. (This works best if you go old-school and use a Polaroid for instant pics.)

YOU'LL NEED:

- A photo for display
- A piece of cardboard (a bit larger than your photo)
- A glue stick
- An assortment of twigs and sticks
- Heavy-duty scissors or pruning shears to cut sticks
- A hot glue gun
- Twine

DIRECTIONS:

1. Start by gluing your photo to the cardboard with the glue stick.
2. Next, arrange the twigs and sticks around the sides of the photo on the edges of the cardboard, cutting them as necessary.
3. Glue the twigs around the edges with a hot glue gun to form the frame. Get creative with how you bundle the sticks together.
4. Once the glue has set, tie or glue the twine around the corners of the frame to put on the finishing touches.

Make Bookmarks

$$\$\,\$\,\$\ |\ \text{\textdagger}+\text{\textdagger\textdagger\textdagger\textdagger}\ |\ \text{\Large\heartsuit}\ \text{\Large\house}$$

What adventure are you going on today? Pick up a book and get started! Not only is reading relaxing, but it takes you into worlds unknown, expanding your mind and keeping you sharp. So let's give books some respect, eh? Instead of dog-earing the page after your nightly read, why not use a bookmark? Make your own as a special camp memory to take home and use with your next good read.

All you'll need is construction paper or card stock, scissors, glue, and big ideas. Start by cutting your construction paper into a 2" × 5" rectangle. Next, get creative in your decorations. You could use your name, designs, patterns, grids—anything goes!

If you have access to a laminating machine it might be a good idea to use that to preserve your work. As an alternative, you can use Mod Podge to seal in the design or cover the bookmark on both sides with clear contact paper.

This is a fun craft to do after a long day of games and competitions when you need some time to relax.

Make Leaf Art

It can be hard to get all those steps in, especially when you feel fatigued or unmotivated. So take a tip from the camp activities director and give your walk a purpose: to gather leaves. You can do this alone, but it's even more fun, and motivating, to round up your kids or a couple of friends and take a walk on the wild side—through the park, down your street, or anywhere you're likely to find fallen leaves. Pick up some of the best examples you can find and bring them home to get creative with leaf art!

Use your imagination to create unique and stunning prints for your home. You'll be able to make something that brings the outdoors in, creates a calming environment, and matches your color scheme. Botanicals are hot!

All you need for this craft is acrylic paint in a variety of colors, heavy paper (such as watercolor paper or card stock), paintbrushes or a printing brayer, and of course, your leaves. Apply paint onto the veiny side of a leaf using the colors of your choice. You can splatter the paint on, drop it on, or use the paintbrushes or brayer to get your desired effect. When you're done painting, place the leaf painted-side down onto your paper. Lay a plain piece of paper on top of the leaf and press firmly but gently over the leaf to ensure all the paint transfers from leaf to paper. Remove the top paper, slowly peel the leaf up, and—voilà—you've created a mini-masterpiece. Hey, you're a natural!

You can use this technique to print cotton fabric for pillows, aprons, place mats, and other home decor items. Substitute fabric paint for the acrylic paint and, after the design dries completely, heat-set the paint by tossing the fabric into a warm dryer for 20 minutes or so or by covering the design with another piece of fabric and running a hot iron over it a few times.

★ PRO TIP ★

Big, sturdy leaves will hold paint the best. Look for leaves that are solid, flat, and not crumbly to avoid a mess in your art. Unless that's what you're going for, Picasso.

Make Sock Puppets

What's cute and never goes out of style? Sock puppets! Yeah, they're silly—that's the point. You can't be sad or depressed when you're making and playing with a sock puppet. Plus, what else are you going to do with all your mismatched and holey socks? Put your imagination to good use and recycle your socks by making a family of sock puppets. Using googly eyes and pieces of felt, you can make these quirky characters come to life!

This is a fun project for a group. Gather your parents and siblings together, craft a few unique puppets, and then put on a show for the little ones in your family. You'll have a blast making a sock puppet version of yourself and planning a show to entertain over Thanksgiving.

Using felt, string, yarn, and even permanent markers, there is so much you can do with a sock puppet. Make the characters from your favorite TV show or from a show the youngsters are watching these days. Just think, you and your sock puppets could be the next *YouTube* sensation. Get your puppet voice ready; it's show time!

Roll with Marble Art

Here's an art project that's as mesmerizing as it is beautiful. To create this cool and unique stylized effect you'll only need acrylic paint, canvas, and marbles!

Start by putting on your artist smock and pour your paint into disposable bowls. Place your marbles in the paint, using a plastic spoon or craft stick to make sure they get covered. Place your canvas on the bottom of a foil-covered baking dish, cardboard box, or serving tray. Drop the marbles on top of the canvas and roll them around. Do it one by one or use multiple marbles at a time. Enjoy the Zen pleasure of watching the marbles make little trails and marks all over the canvas. You'll be left with a textured effect the brings a new dimension to your art! Go with neon for a bright, fun look or pick earth tones to really bring in the warmth. When the paint is dry, heat-set the paint by putting it in a warm dryer for about 20 minutes or by covering the design with a cloth and running a hot iron over it several times. Then frame your masterpiece or cut it up and stitch it with additional fabric to make a pillow, coasters, a book cover, or whatever strikes your fancy.

Emboss Nature Stones

Here's a way to cast your camp memories in stone, so to speak. Nature "stones" are made with air-drying clay, natural objects, and paint. This craft engages your senses, from scavenging for objects in nature to exploring textures, to softening the clay in your hands and making the prints. It is a fun and contemplative craft that can be useful.

Gather your natural objects. You'll want to select items that have some texture and are fairly firm: acorn tops, pinecones, sturdy leaves and flowers, sticks, seed pods, and shells make good choices, but use your imagination.

Take a golf-ball-sized amount of air-drying clay and soften it up by kneading it with your hands. Shape it into a rounded, flattened shape resembling a smooth stone. Now take an object and press it into the clay to make an impression. You can make one impression or press repeatedly over the top of the clay to make a pattern. If you don't like what you've done, just rework the clay in your hands until it's smooth again and redo the print.

Make as many stones as you like, then let them air-dry overnight. When dry, they will be very lightweight. Paint with acrylic paints, using colors or metallic gold or silver. The stones can be arranged together for display; you can glue them to a frame, a card, or other pieces of artwork; or you can glue a magnet on the back. This is an easy project to make with kids or elders, and the stones make great little party favors.

PART 7
THE GREAT ESCAPE

This is the moment you finally get to just get away from it all and focus on *you*. Sometimes all the responsibilities that come with being an adult are purely overwhelming. Adulting is hard! With bills to pay and people needing something from you left and right, no one can blame you for trying to carve out some much-needed "me" time. When life is too much to handle and you feel like tossing in the towel, throw it back to the days when you could hide in a blanket fort and block out the world. You hereby have my permission to take a nap and give yourself a break!

Creating calm moments within your day will help you relax after a long stressful week. By disconnecting from the world and removing pressure from yourself, you can enjoy your own company. No phones allowed! With these chill-out activities, you'll be relaxed in no time. And let's be real, a little comfort food doesn't hurt either! This is truly the great escape you've been needing. Right this way...

Build a Blanket Fort

Spending the day building a cozy blanket fort and camping out inside for a few hours is a great way to shut out the world and just relax!

Pull together some chairs or furniture from around your home. Grab all the cozy blankets and pillows that you can find and get to work. Position your furniture slightly less wide than your biggest blanket. You can use something tall like a broom handle or a taller piece of furniture to hold up the middle of the blanket in tentlike fashion. If necessary, use heavy objects such as books to hold down the edges of the blanket, keeping them from slipping out of place.

Now it's time to load up your fort with all the cozy things! Toss in the blankets, pillows, and even your childhood stuffed animals that I know are hiding out in your room somewhere. Bring in your computer to watch *Netflix*, bring a book, or simply just bring yourself. This is your safe space to relax in and let go of all the pressure you've been under.

Only furry friends allowed. Don't forget the snacks!

Read Your Favorite Childhood Books

There's nothing like settling into your favorite reading nook with a hot latte and snuggling up with a good read. Hunker down for an hour with your old copies of *Harry Potter and the Sorcerer's Stone* or *The Little Prince* and remind yourself of how magical a book can be!

These novels bring back wonderful memories of story time before it was lights out. Whether you're revisiting the book your mom always read to you or the first book you borrowed from the library, these stories teach us valuable lessons that really shape us as we grow up. With story lines that remind us of the virtues of forgiveness, kindness, respect, and that instill a sense of adventure, these classics will always have a special place in our hearts.

If you don't have your favorite books on hand or in storage somewhere, zip down to your local library and page through a few books in the children's section. You might even come across books you had forgotten about. And if you feel silly reading a children's book, find a young person to read to. If you don't have a relative the right age, babysit a friend's child or volunteer at a school.

Play Dress Up

$$$ | 👤+👤👤👤👤 | 🌳 🏠

Dressing up and trying new styles is a great way to play pretend. Step out of your professional skirts and blouses, suits, or hoodies and jeans and explore new options! Take a trip to the thrift shop and pick out a few things to try. This is your chance to find out if you really look good in plaid shirts or a leather jacket. Maybe you wouldn't actually wear a beaded prom dress in public, but it's fun to check it out in the dressing room. And you know, maybe you'd go out more if you owned your own tuxedo.

Purchase a few things (most thrift shop finds won't break the bank) and take them home. Mix and match with your old wardrobe and see what combinations your inner Tim Gunn can create.

I challenge you to create a board of style inspiration from your favorite celebrities, political figures, style bloggers, or role models. The clothes we wear can make a huge impact on our confidence! If we know we look good, we feel good as well. If you have a big presentation coming up at work, try emulating the style of your favorite power broker. Spend some time in your new outfit practicing that presentation in your living room. I guarantee you will find all the confidence you need to nail it.

Make Believe with Barbie

Dress them up and play make believe as you mime them through scenarios with their friends and drive them around in their convertibles. Barbie and Skipper's dream house is just waiting to put your decorating skills to work. Spend a Saturday afternoon throwing it back to the days spent on your bedroom floor making up stories for your Barbie dolls. Planning out their lives was much simpler than planning out your own!

Raid your parents' attic to find the dolls you used to play with or check out a nearby toy store for the new releases in Barbie's world. You'll be inspired by the diversity of the dolls of today as compared to Barbie's first release in 1959. Barbie has evolved in not only the shape of her body but in her career paths as well. She can really be anything she wants to be! Playing with Barbies is a fun rainy day activity if you have young nieces and nephews who are interested in playing make-believe. As it turns out, she's an icon for more than her looks.

Not into Barbie? How about Star Wars action figures, Transformers, or even a bag full of green army men? Any of those will keep you busy inventing scenarios and strategies for hours.

POP TRIVIA

Barbie's full name is actually Barbara Millicent Roberts. She's had over eighty careers including news anchor, pilot, veterinarian, and Canadian Mountie. You go, girl!

Make Grilled Cheese Sandwiches

There's nothing like the comfort of a deliciously gooey grilled cheese sandwich! Warm and toasty, homemade grilled cheese is sure to hit the spot. Pair your grilled cheese with a classic bowl of tomato soup. It's the perfect match for the cheesy goodness you just made and great for winter evenings.

MAKES 1 SERVING

YOU'LL NEED:

- 2 pieces bread (type of your choice)
- $1/2$–1 tablespoon butter
- 2 slices cheese (sharp Cheddar or creamy, rich cheeses such as Gouda, Brie, or goat cheese will suit your grown-up palate)
- Optional: $1/2$ tablespoon cream cheese

DIRECTIONS:

1. Heat a frying pan over medium heat.
2. Butter one side of each slice of bread.
3. When the pan is hot, lay one piece of bread buttered side down.
4. Put the cheese slices on top. Allow them to melt slightly around the edges.
5. Optional: spread the cream cheese on the non-buttered side on the remaining piece of bread.
6. Place the remaining piece of bread buttered side up on top of the cheese.
7. Check the bottom piece of bread by lifting the edge of the sandwich slightly with a spatula. If it is browned, it is ready to turn over.
8. Flip the sandwich to allow the second piece of bread to cook and reach your desired level of crispiness.
9. After 2–3 minutes, remove the sandwich from the pan. Time to eat!

Commune with Nature

Spending a Saturday morning outdoors and getting your body moving is an awesome way to take in the calming effects of nature to relieve stress. Even if your general reaction to nature is like Meredith from *The Parent Trap* (the one with Lindsay Lohan, thank you), you'll still find peace in getting outside. Not to mention the air quality in a forest or on a walking path is often much better than being surrounded by concrete. While you tramp through the forest, those plants and trees are doing their thing to create fresh oxygen, making your thoughts clearer and your world brighter!

When you go on a nature walk, your goal is not to reach a destination. The point of this type of activity is to reconnect with the world around you and discover with wonder. It's not the destination, it's the journey! We get caught up in the hustle and bustle of everyday life and often forget to learn new things, stop and appreciate the world for what it is, and express gratitude. Getting back to nature will re-center you in no time.

Pick a local path that works well for your fitness level, preferably in a park or safe wooded area. Something mild with little incline will be perfect for this activity. Give yourself an hour or two to meander along the path. Keep your phone on silent in your pocket—no checking it or listening to music while you're on this hike! Notice the animals and what they are doing. Look around at the foliage and levels of life and decay. Not to get too philosophical here, but pay attention to the cyclical energy around you—it will calm you, inspire you, and motivate you—all in one go.

Fly a Kite

Heading out to fly a kite on a lightly breezy day is the perfect way to relax! Grab a kite and set off into a field, park, beach, or other relatively empty area away from power lines, buildings, or trees and just let it go! It's a peaceful activity that people of all ages can take part in.

Keep in mind that flying a kite is like Goldilocks—conditions have to be just right for it to soar! Too little wind and your kite won't take off; too much wind and you won't be able to control the kite. Check the weather and head out on the next lightly breezy day. Embrace the sense of tranquility and freedom and even learn to do a trick or two.

You could fly a kite with friends, of course, but there is something so peaceful about going out by yourself. You're learning something new and creating a meditative experience for yourself. Don't stress about it. It's okay if it's not smooth sailing for you and your kite. The most important thing is that you're trying. I bet you'll have that kite flying in no time!

POP TRIVIA

The Guinness World Record for the highest altitude a kite has ever been flown is 16,009'. Wow!

Finger Paint

Get messy with this hands-on approach to art as you tickle your creative nerve and create something beautiful. Use this go-to craft to refine your motor skills and relax your worries away. The best thing about using your fingers is that it doesn't have to be perfect! Allow yourself to create and paint outside of the lines.

Simply putting finger to paper is freeing in the best way possible. It's a chance for you to do whatever the heck you want.

You can be as messy or as clean as you like with your finger painting (it's you who is going to have to clean up the mess, after all). Paint and paper made especially for finger painting are best, because they are made to be slippery and slick, respectively, the better to slide your fingers around. However, you can use acrylic craft paint and freezer paper or any paper with a smooth, nonporous finish. You'll soon find that your fingers gliding through the smooth and silky paint is so satisfying and calming.

Don't stress if you don't make something Louvre-worthy. You're creating just for you—no one needs to see what you've made and it's okay if it goes right into the recycling bin. It's the process that's important. If you're happy with how it turns out, hang it on your refrigerator and display it for the world to see. With red, yellow, and blue—there's no limit to what you can do!

Make Grown-Up Root Beer Floats

Creamy vanilla ice cream mixed with dark, foamy root beer makes for a delicious afternoon delight. Add a bit of bourbon and you have yourself a grown-up root beer float!

MAKES 1 SERVING

YOU'LL NEED:

- $1/2$ cup whole-milk vanilla ice cream
- 1 ounce bourbon
- $1/2$–$3/4$ cup old-fashioned root beer (in a glass bottle if you can find it)
- Whipped cream to taste

DIRECTIONS:

1. Put your serving glass in the freezer at least 2 hours before you plan to make your root beer float.
2. Add the ice cream to the glass.
3. Pour in the bourbon. Add the root beer immediately after, being careful not to let the foam overfill the glass.
4. Top with whipped cream and serve immediately. Tasty!

Keep a Diary

$$$ | 👤👤👤👤+ | 🌳🏠

Diaries aren't just for middle school crushes and drama! Spilling your guts to your diary is the next best thing to talking with your girlfriends over brunch. Truthfully, making decisions is hard! Writing about them brings us clarity about the things we deal with that bring us stress and anxiety. Oh, and we're gonna go analog on this—you'll be writing by hand in a book—no digital diaries. Why? Because studies show handwriting engages your brain more than typing on a keyboard, improving long-term retention, better thought organization, and an increased ability to generate ideas.

One way to keep up with your diary is to freewrite. Freewriting is a technique where you simply set a timer for 10–20 minutes and just let out whatever comes to mind. You might write about your day, start a work of fiction, relive your best childhood memories, or anything else your heart desires! Letting your mind just wander and spilling thoughts out onto a page is a great way to declutter your mind and unlock your creativity.

If freewriting isn't for you, write letters to your future self or treat your diary like a friend. This is a safe space where you can say anything you want. Be yourself!

Watch Saturday Morning Cartoons

When was the last time you actually got up early on a Saturday morning? Not to mention early enough to watch cartoons? There's no better way to feel like a kid—and free of responsibilities—than kicking back and relaxing with an early morning bowl of cereal and a heaping helping of laughs (plus a very grown-up dose of caffeine), while still in your jammies.

The best part is, nowadays you aren't limited by what's on "regular" TV. Stream some old episodes of your favorite Nickelodeon classics from the early 2000s such as *Rugrats*, *SpongeBob SquarePants*, *The Fairly OddParents*, *Rocket Power*, *As Told by Ginger*, and more. Relive the magic of Saturday morning before the day gets going. This is a cool tradition to start with your family now as well, especially if you have little kids! Pancakes, anyone?

Jump Rope

Jumping rope is a fun way to relieve stress and challenge yourself! If you feel like I'm tricking you into exercising, hear me out. Put your coordination to the test as you spin the jump rope around overhead and hop up just in time to miss tripping all over yourself! Getting your heart rate up and getting your cardio in is just a welcome bonus.

Spend a few minutes every day practicing your timing and you'll be a pro in no time. Start off easy—jumping rope really is a challenging exercise and is actually often added as a conditioning element to workouts as a test of agility and speed! Jumping regularly has numerous benefits including increased bone mineral density.

Put on some music or set a timer for a minute and see how many jumps you can get in. Test yourself every day to see how you're improving over time. Just like with dancing, you'll be moving your way to a better you. You'll burn some calories, improve your balance, and improve your overall health. All while doing a "kid's" activity. Sounds like a win-win-win to me!

FUN FOR EVERYONE:
You can jump rope with friends too! Pull out the rhymes of your youth, such as "Miss Mary Mack," "Teddy Bear, Teddy Bear," or "Cinderella" and see who can jump the longest.

Listen to Records

It's totally rad to be able to listen to your favorite jams on surround sound, but there's nothing quite like the smooth tone of a record player. From the sound quality to the physical act of putting the records on and taking them off, listening to records is a complete experience that you just don't get with your iPod. Kids these days! They don't know what they're missing.

Ask your parents if you can sort through their vinyl or head down to a local music shop. Most places still sell records. You'll feel like you stepped back in time when you set one of those babies on the turntable.

Turn the lights off and burn some candles. This sets the mood perfectly for some quality "me" time. Pure bliss.

Write in a Journal

Who doesn't love a good Q&A session? In your journal, the spotlight is on you! While it's similar to writing in a diary, journaling involves following very specific prompts and questions that put your killer writing skills to good use.

Here are a few journaling prompts to get you started:

- Create your dream job
- Write a haiku about your bedroom
- Describe your perfect day
- Explain your dream house in detail
- Share a time when you were most proud of yourself
- List ten things you are grateful for right now
- Summarize your favorite book
- Describe your strengths in detail
- Write a poem about your favorite outfit
- Pen a letter to your favorite relative

Go ahead, treat yourself to a beautiful journal (you only have to use a composition book if you really want to) and schedule time into your day to get your journal on!

Take a Bubble Bath

$ $ $ | ♀♀♀♀♀ + | 🌳 🏠

Back before there were bath bombs, Mr. Bubble totally ruled the tub scene! That adorable pink bottle and iconic bubble gum scent were pure joy for kids all across America.

Run yourself a warm bath and treat yourself to a relaxing dip. It's the perfect opportunity to catch up on some reading or listen to some music! The joy of a few moments to yourself is a gift that should be treasured. Ah, I feel more relaxed already.

BLAST FROM THE PAST

Mr. Bubble has released a luxury line of products that includes bath salts, body soaks, cocoa butter bars, bath bombs, and more. And yes, it's available in the classic bubble gum scent.

Have Cereal for Dinner

I know you're trying to be healthy with your dinner of grilled chicken, roasted vegetables, and brown rice. (And really, go you!) But when you've had a long day and you can't even keep your eyes open, sometimes there's nothing more comforting than the meals of our childhood.

True, having cereal for dinner is a bit rebellious. But throw caution to the wind! You're an adult now. We're having cereal for dinner and no one can stop us.

I'm not talking about eating your Wheaties, either. No ma'am, not tonight. Not on my watch. Since you're doing the grocery shopping around these parts, take this as permission to eat whichever sugar-laden cereal you're craving.

Growing up, cereal for dinner might have been a last resort for tired parents who didn't have the energy to cook a "real" meal, but now, cereal is a simple comfort food. It's easy to make (seriously, it's just cereal and milk), requires minimal clean up (put that bowl and spoon in the dishwasher), and leaves you with a full belly that can get ready for bed. What more could you want?

Create a Candy Stash

Raise your hand if you had a major sweet tooth growing up. Kids today are really missing out on the joys of the novelty candy we had in the '70s, '80s, and '90s, aren't they? There were some really creative things on the market in those decades!

Some of these candies are still readily available and can be purchased at your local grocery store. For others, you might have to search for specialty candy shops or look on the Internet to find the hidden treasures of your youth.

These sweet treats are probably what you used to spend your allowance on, so why not reminisce a little bit and see if they're what you remember? Here's a list of common candies from childhoods gone by:

- Ring Pops
- Fun Dip
- Lemonhead
- Warheads
- Big League Chew
- Now and Later
- Laffy Taffy
- Runts
- Junior Mints
- AirHeads
- 100 Grand
- Banana Split Candy Chews
- Broadway Rolls
- Candy bracelets and necklaces
- Pixy Stix
- Blow Pops
- Bottle Caps

- Bubble Yum
- Cherryheads
- Gobstoppers
- Jelly Belly Soda Pop Bottle
- Pop Rocks
- Rock candy
- Root Beer Floats
- Smarties
- Whistle Pops
- Caramello
- Cow Tales
- Chupa Chups
- Push Pops
- Baby Bottle Pops
- Peach Rings
- Nerds Rope
- Sour Punch Twists
- Wonder Ball

·FUN FOR EVERYONE·

Remember "penny candy"? It costs a bit more now, but there are still places where you can go in and pick out your favorite candies, one at a time, from fishbowl glass jars. To keep yourself from going wild, set a limit— say two bucks—and ration out your selections accordingly. Let's see, I'll have two gumballs, three Nik-L-Nips, one Blow Pop...

Is your favorite on this list? On your next trip to the grocery store, make a pit stop between the produce aisle and the organic milks to check out the candy selection. Your secret stash is safe with me!

Color

Putting pencil to paper and coloring within the lines is a relaxing way to end your evening. Instead of watching TV, pick up an adult coloring book and shade your worries away. Coloring books for adults can be purchased almost anywhere with any theme. Whether it's Harry Potter, superheroes, or a flower garden that's more your style, there's something for everything. (And, you know, if you want a My Little Pony coloring book from the kids' section, that's totally okay. You do you.)

Coloring is quite a therapeutic activity and is often recommended for people who struggle with anxiety. Use it as a way to untangle your thoughts and free your mind by opening up a creative outlet. And the truth is, anyone can color! All it takes are some colored pencils, crayons, or markers, and you're good to go.

If you come home from work feeling exhausted and you know that cup of coffee at 3 p.m. barely did anything to perk you up, pick up your coloring book and go with the flow. Coloring distracts you just enough to relax, but you'll still feel accomplished at the beautiful artwork you completed. Set your mind free!

Make Your Own Lunchables

Remember those preassembled meal kits that came in yellow packets? Back in the day, there were options like pepperoni pizza, mini hot dogs, and turkey and ham sandwiches. If you were lucky, yours came with a Reese's Peanut Butter Cup or Oreos and a Capri Sun. As basic as they were, you definitely felt like royalty opening that packet. Since you're already making your own lunch, why not make it fun and do meal prep Lunchables style?

Get yourself a few bento boxes (Japanese containers that have separate compartments for different items of food) and prepare your own Lunchables. Chop up your veggies and pack your dressing for a salad. Add a wrap for a variation. Put in all the ingredients for mini-pizzas or do turkey and cheese roll-ups. Even last night's leftovers are more fun in these little compartments. Make Gordon Ramsay proud!

Oh, and make sure you include something from your candy stash. A little treat goes a long way.

?? POP TRIVIA ??

Lunchables were first released in 1988 exclusively in Seattle before being distributed internationally starting in 1989. The more you know!

Go Cloud Watching

$ $ $ | 🧍 + 🧍🧍🧍🧍 | 🌳 🏠

Is it a shark? Is it a bear? What do you see in that cloud passing over-head? Head out on a warm, dry day and pick a soft spot where you have a clear view of the sky. Bring a blanket and your imagination and lie back and watch the clouds roll on by.

When you look up, what do you see? There are no wrong answers here—it's the thought that counts. Use your imagination and don't judge! Allow yourself to be inspired by the nature that floats above you.

While you're at it, take some time to recall your elementary school cloud formation lessons. You probably remember the basics like the fluffy white ones are called cumulus clouds and rain clouds are of the nimbus variety. What about more unique cloud phenomena like wave clouds and arcus clouds? Would you recognize them if you saw them? Cloud watching is fun to do with your own kids too. Just call yourself Ms. Frizzle or Bill Nye the Science Guy.

Go Stargazing

Remember when you were a little kid and first noticed the moon? How magical it seemed. Or, when you first learned how to find the Big Dipper or Orion's Belt? Nowadays, you may not even notice these celestial wonders. But they're still there, waiting for you to look up. So, it's time to go stargazing! If it's cold, bundle up with a jacket, sit outside on your deck or lie on the lawn, and look up into a galaxy far, far away. Check the Internet for celestial happenings such as the Perseid meteor shower (every August) or a lunar eclipse. If possible, get far away from city and suburban lights. You'll be amazed at how many stars you can see with the naked eye when you're truly in the dark. You could even buy yourself a telescope or visit an observatory on a personal field trip to discover more about the stars, planets, and our galaxy.

People have been gazing upwards toward the sky for millennia, and for all sorts of reasons. The stars have been used as directional tools for navigators all across the planet. Ships have sailed through seas unknown based on these galactic markers. The calendars and timetables that we live by are based on the astronomical cycles of the sun and the moon. And the constellations are essential in zodiac interpretations of sun and moon signs that have been guiding humankind in decision-making through the ages. Needless to say, the night sky plays a major role in human expansion across the globe.

To benefit from stargazing you don't even need to know all the constellations or even anything about light-years. Even if you've forgotten the specifics, it's fascinating to see what is happening in our skies during the time we sleep every night.

Rock Out with a Playlist

Jam out to the boy bands of your younger years! Let those bittersweet melodies take you back to the carefree moments when you sang your heart out (even if it was a little out of tune). Break out your playlist while you clean your house or play it in the background while you work out and get your heart rate up. Put together your favorite songs from the groups that sang the sound track to your high school years. These jams will bring back sweet memories of the songs you almost forgot about and put you in the best mood ever!

Take a Nap

Lie back in your chair, curl up on a couch, or snooze in your car for a few minutes—it's nap time, people! Even just a 20-minute power nap is enough to refresh your mind and focus for the afternoon ahead.

We really didn't know how good we had it as kids, did we? Now, though, come two in the afternoon, a nap sounds like the most rejuvenating thing in the world. So why not indulge yourself every now and then? It sure beats out yet another cup of coffee!

If you can, try napping in a cooler, quiet environment. The cooler temperatures help put your body into sleep mode. Even if you're not able to fall asleep, a few minutes of peace and quiet can be equally effective in boosting your mood. Put it into your schedule and set your phone to "do not disturb"—this is your time.

Your afternoon catnap will give you the boost of energy you need to power through the rest of your day. Just in case you need another reason to stretch out and catch some zzz's, short naps can also be especially helpful if you haven't been sleeping well enough at night. Naps allow you to catch up on your sleep debt before any major side effects show up. Yawn. I think I'm going to go take my nap now. Shh...

Blow Bubble Art

Blowing bubbles and watching them turn into little floating rainbows that move away in the wind is so relaxing. It's the perfect activity for a spring day. Plus, it's fun to chase and pop bubbles! Take it to the next level and turn your bubbly passion into a masterpiece for your home with bubble art.

Making bubble art is a piece of cake! Add a few drops of watercolor paint to your bubble mix. Use a few colors for a cool rainbow effect. Dip your bubble wand into the mix and blow toward a canvas. As the bubbles reach the paper and pop, you'll create an ethereal and understated design you won't find at the home store! Nothing says "welcome home" like a unique piece of art!

★ PRO TIP ★

Pair bubbles with bubbly and treat yourself to a glass of champagne while you make your art!

US/METRIC CONVERSION CHART

VOLUME CONVERSIONS

US Volume Measure	Metric Equivalent
⅛ teaspoon	0.5 milliliter
¼ teaspoon	1 milliliter
½ teaspoon	2 milliliters
1 teaspoon	5 milliliters
½ tablespoon	7 milliliters
1 tablespoon (3 teaspoons)	15 milliliters
2 tablespoons (1 fluid ounce)	30 milliliters
¼ cup (4 tablespoons)	60 milliliters
⅓ cup	80 milliliters
½ cup (4 fluid ounces)	125 milliliters
⅔ cup	160 milliliters
¾ cup (6 fluid ounces)	180 milliliters
1 cup (16 tablespoons)	250 milliliters
1 pint (2 cups)	500 milliliters
1 quart (4 cups)	1 liter (about)

WEIGHT CONVERSIONS

US Weight Measure	Metric Equivalent
½ ounce	15 grams
1 ounce	30 grams
2 ounces	60 grams
3 ounces	85 grams
¼ pound (4 ounces)	115 grams
½ pound (8 ounces)	225 grams
¾ pound (12 ounces)	340 grams
1 pound (16 ounces)	454 grams

OVEN TEMPERATURE CONVERSIONS

Degrees Fahrenheit	Degrees Celsius
200 degrees F	95 degrees C
250 degrees F	120 degrees C
275 degrees F	135 degrees C
300 degrees F	150 degrees C
325 degrees F	160 degrees C
350 degrees F	180 degrees C
375 degrees F	190 degrees C
400 degrees F	205 degrees C
425 degrees F	220 degrees C
450 degrees F	230 degrees C

BAKING PAN SIZES

American	Metric
8 × 1½ inch round baking pan	20 × 4 cm cake tin
9 × 1½ inch round baking pan	23 × 3.5 cm cake tin
11 × 7 × 1½ inch baking pan	28 × 18 × 4 cm baking tin
13 × 9 × 2 inch baking pan	30 × 20 × 5 cm baking tin
2 quart rectangular baking dish	30 × 20 × 3 cm baking tin
15 × 10 × 2 inch baking pan	38 × 25 × 5 cm baking tin (Swiss roll tin)
9 inch pie plate	22 × 4 or 23 × 4 cm pie plate
7 or 8 inch springform pan	18 or 20 cm springform or loose bottom cake tin
9 × 5 × 3 inch loaf pan	23 × 13 × 7 cm or 2 lb narrow loaf or pâté tin
1½ quart casserole	1.5 liter casserole
2 quart casserole	2 liter casserole

INDEX